"M*A*S*h" series, as well as for several motion pictures.

With candid insight, wit, and perception, the author discusses the pitfalls of writing a weekly series, of dealing with the television actor's "injustice syndrome," and of revamping existing series to beef up ratings or to accommodate cast changes. A compelling portrait of Wally Cox, and forthright asides on David Susskind, George Gobel, Walter Brennan, Alan Alda, McLean Stevenson, and Marlon Brando illuminate the many facets of Everett Greenbaum's engaging, always fascinating life.

The Goldenberg Who Couldn't Dance

EVERETT GREENBAUM

The Goldenberg Who Couldn't Dance

HARCOURT BRACE JOVANOVICH　　NEW YORK AND LONDON

Copyright © 1973, 1975, 1976, 1980 by Everett Greenbaum

All rights reserved. No part of
this publication may be reproduced or
transmitted in any form or by any means,
electronic or mechanical, including photocopy,
recording, or any information storage and
retrieval system, without permission
in writing from the publisher.

Requests for permission to make copies of
any part of the work should be mailed to:
Permissions, Harcourt Brace Jovanovich, Inc.
757 Third Avenue, New York, N.Y. 10017

Portions of "A Dollar of My Own" are reprinted with
permission from The Saturday Evening Post Company. © 1967
The Curtis Publishing Company, © 1978 The Saturday Evening
Post Company. An early version of "The Prince of the Yellow
Perils" appeared in *Private Pilot*, 1975. Portions of "Making the
Rounds," "The Day I Killed Weintraub," and "Trouble in
Jefferson City" appeared in *Performing Arts*, Los Angeles.

Library of Congress Cataloging in Publication Data

Greenbaum, Everett.
   The Goldenberg who couldn't dance.

   1. Greenbaum, Everett—Biography.   2. Screen writers—
United States—Biography.   I. Title.
PS3557.R3763.465   812'.54 [B]   79-3353
ISBN 0-15-136174-6

Printed in the United States of America
Set in CRT Baskerville
First edition
B C D E

To my wife,
who brought me peace,
serenity, and order,
and to the memory of Jim Fritzell

Contents

Arson in the Spring	1
A Dollar of My Own	7
Just Bring in an Honest Face	13
The Candy King	19
Taking Off	27
The Prince of the Yellow Perils	35
Majuro	39
Making the Rounds	55
A *Débutant* in Paris	59
Good Evening, Friends of Radio in the Greater Buffalo Area	79
The Day I Killed Weintraub	89
Wally	101
Chipping Away	111
Trouble in Jefferson City	119
Hello, Hollywood, Hello	131
Adventures in the Laugh Trade	141
The Years in El Dorado	151

Arson
in the Spring

Of my mother and the other Goldenberg sisters, Uncle Arthur used to say, "Ain't none of them Vassar."
All blue-eyed and fair, the most *shiksa* was Aunt Leah, Uncle Arthur's wife. When Aunt Leah threw her golf clubs into the rumble seat of their Dodge coupe, you'd swear it was Ginger Rogers.
One spring afternoon when I was four, Aunt Leah came to Buffalo for a visit. My bath was over. Upstairs Mamma and Winnie Saint-Cleveland were bathing the girls. Until recently we had been bathed together but I was starting to ask questions.
"Why don't I look like the girls between the legs?" I asked Winnie Saint-Cleveland.

"Well, they has their Maggies and you has your Jiggs," she explained.

"But why don't we all have the same thing there?"

Winnie Saint-Cleveland thought a while. Then she said, "It's because you is sick."

I worried about this but soon got to enjoying my guys-only bath.

On this particular day I was finished with bathing and had been put into my pongee suit. I went downstairs. Aunt Leah was brushing my hair, humming to the new roll on the Ampico Player Piano.

" 'Do do do what you done done done befooooooooore . . . baby.' "

"Ouch!" I said. "You're pulling."

"Combs pull, not brushes, you nut." She took a good look at me. "You know what, kid? You look like a regular sheik."

It was nice to have Aunt Leah visit but it interfered with my usual after-bath routine . . . going into the cellar to play with matches.

" 'Do do do what you done done done . . .' Dance with me, Ev." She picked me up.

"I can't dance."

"Don't be silly. There is no such thing as a Goldenberg who can't dance."

She hummed and sang and twirled around with me until the roll finished and began flapping in the piano. Then she dropped onto the couch to read the new *Cosmo* before her afternoon snooze. For a while, I went out on the back porch. The day smelled of dandelions, warm grass, and new shingles on the house next to Saint Mark's. I munched on a piece of matzoh, watching bumblebees, until Aunt Leah fell asleep. Then I slipped into the cellar.

The matches, the big jobs with blue-and-white tips, were kept up on top of the black machine that turned the furnace on and off. You got them down by pulling a chair over and reaching with your father's old niblick. One scratch on the sandy side of the matchbox and there would be sizzling, a flame, and a firecracker smell. Very nice! Then, just before the flames reached your fingers, you dropped the match in the wet drainage ditch along the cellar floor. It sputtered out. "Splut!"

I pulled the chair over to get the matches. Upstairs I could hear Winnie Saint-Cleveland singing a Jesus song as she soaped the girls.

I couldn't remember a time when Winnie wasn't there, because she arrived before I was born. I figured her to be a black relative.

We were very close. She called me her boy. After dinner each night, I went into the kitchen to visit while she ate her dinner. She gave me fried chicken skin she called "grievings," and sassafras tea. She told me about her religion . . . how she'd gotten sanctified at church by the Spirit knocking her down to the floor.

There were lots of interesting things about Winnie. One was that over her hair, which was soaked in tar oil, she wore a wig which looked much the same as her hair. The oil gave her a swell aroma, redolent of the truck that came around to fix the street. Razor blades loomed large in her legend. She used them to trim corns. Her ex-husband had used them on her, leaving little train tracks on her funny-sad face. She had many sayings. One was for the beach.

"Nobody should see a woman in a bathing suit 'cept her husband or her doctor."

If you asked her for the time, she would say, "Time all dogs is dead. Ain't you sick?"

On the subject of punching your sisters, she presented her version of a warning from my father. "You hits a girl in the stomach. The ambulance comes and that's all there is to it."

When talking pictures came in and people told her about them, she would say, "They makin' fools of you. They got people back there."

But this day, while Winnie and Mamma were bathing the girls, and Aunt Leah visiting from Philly was asleep on the couch, I was in the cellar with a flaming match in my hand.

The water in the ditch had dried up.

My fingers were getting hot. I dropped the match. Then, to be doubly sure it went out, I dumped a bushel basket of old rags and papers over it. This worked fine for about five seconds; then, with a "whoosh," the bushel basket belched out a tower of flame. Then . . . panic. I headed up the stairs. In the dining room was a built-in, glass-doored china closet containing a little silver carpet sweeper for sweeping crumbs off the table, two silver pigeons, and English china cups, animals, and people, brought over from Canada on the ferryboat. I stopped to stare.

The wood flooring in front of this repository was smoking and turning black. Glass panes in the door, heating up, began to pop out, shattering as they hit the floor. Seeing family treasures, solid, dependable possessions, go to pieces worried me.

A tin chute ran from the bathroom to the laundry bin in the cellar, but even without the chute Mamma would have smelled smoke. It was one of the things she did better than anybody. She'd already sent Winnie down to look.

"Fire!" Winnie screamed, about an inch from my ear. "Fire, Lord Jesus, fire!"

The girls were wrapped in turkish towels. Aunt Leah was still in her housecoat as we streamed across the lawn to the Egberts' next door, all yelling "Fire!"

"I'm going back in!" Mamma turned back to the fire. "My New York fur. My Chicago ring!"

"Now, Mrs. Greenbaum." Mrs. Egbert took her arm. "Those are only things. They aren't worth it."

Everyone always listened to Mrs. Egbert. She was an actual Wellesley grad. She understood psychology. When Mamma caught a person playing doctor with Irene Egbert there was a whipping. When that same person was caught by Mrs. Egbert, there were cookies.

Education is a wonderful thing.

The big red-and-brass fire engines arrived in no time at all. Sirens, lights. Hoses flopped down onto the street filling with water. Still in my pongee suit, hair still brushed, cheeks blazing hot, I stood on the Egberts' veranda, torn between fascination and guilt.

"I did it. I started the fire," I told a passing fireman.

"I did it," I told Jackie Egbert, who was three.

"I did it," I told Mamma, who had escaped from Mrs. Egbert and was being dragged out of our house by a policeman.

There was a blasting of horns, a yelping of brakes, as my father pulled up in his green Pierce Arrow. He leaped out, running toward me.

Here was my chance at expiation.

"I did it, Daddy. I started the fire." I held out my palm. "Here, hit my hand."

He picked me up and hugged me. Luckily, someone had told him I was trapped in the cellar.

While the house was rebuilt, we visited Philadelphia and Daddy lived at his club.

A Dollar
of My Own

My father, Alexander Greenbaum, was a serious and ambitious man. Like my mother, he was born in Philadelphia. His parents died when I was in my early teens. Grandma Greenbaum, I remember, hung her own wallpaper and on weekends kept a huge live carp in the bathtub. Grandpop Greenbaum never smiled and spent most of his time in the basement making lamps out of empty World War One shells.

Even as a small boy, their son Al was known as "the gentleman sport." Though they were poor, he wore a tie and jacket. In high school he began wearing starched collars. His great obsession was commerce. Retailing was his destiny.

When he was only six, he went into the pretzel business. He bought pretzels for a penny, put salt on them, and sold the salted pretzels for two pennies.

"All I want is a dollar of my own," he was reported to have said.

When he was eleven, he expanded the pretzel business to include renting folding chairs at parades. Philadelphia had plenty of parades then. An older boy began renting umbrellas. Then he added folding chairs to his line and told my father to get lost. Little Al grabbed one of the umbrellas, fractured the older boy's skull with it, and made the territory his for good.

"I play to win" was his motto.

At fifteen he managed to open a nickelodeon. He took money at the door, ran the projector, and did the film rewinding himself. Business was fair, but he made a bad decision. "The movie business will never amount to nothing. It don't signify," he said, closing down the nickelodeon.

Eventually he became a high-school grad ... the first of his family in the new world. He was peacock-proud of his graduation certificate.

"You don't need a thing more than this unless you go for doctor or dentist," he said.

While he and Mamma were "keeping company" in Philadelphia, he was bitten by the tire bug.

His older sister, Sarah, was married to a man who owned a small factory that manufactured auto tires. The tire treads spelled out their trademark, "EVERGRIP." As you drove down a dirt road the tires stamped out their own advertising: EVERGRIP EVERGRIP EVERGRIP in the mud.

So Dad went to work for his brother-in-law Phil Malickson, selling the EVERGRIPs through the mail to farmers, and for a while everything went smoothly. Then all the EVERGRIP tires all over the country began to go bad. They began to unroll, leaving thousands of angry farmers all over the country waving huge EVERGRIP rubber stamps in the direction of Philadelphia. Phil went out of business.

By this time, however, Al had tires in his blood. There was no turning back. Now engaged to Mamma, he had saved up enough money to start in a business of his own. He wrote to the Chambers of Commerce of twenty cities. One city answered. Buffalo ... "Queen City of the Lakes" ... a little bit of Siberia by the sea. He told Mamma, his fiancée, to wait, and took the Pennsy north.

He rented one of these little half-number addresses on Main Street, and worked fourteen hours a day, changing the tires himself, taking small, junky-looking ads in the papers to attract tire bargain hunters. For a while things were slow. Then one day he got an inspiration. At first, like many innovations throughout history, it seemed madness. But it became the basis for the future of "Motor Tire Supply Company."

It was simply stated.

Why not sell tires on credit to Polish people? And Italian and black and regular people too?

In no time at all this caught on. He invented a catchy phrase which was painted on the storefront and appeared in all the advertising: EASY CREDIT. JUST BRING IN AN HONEST FACE.

Henry Hearn came down the street one day, stopped to talk tires, and became the first employee. Soon, with the help of Henry and another employee, Eddie Ziffle, things were running well. It was time to take a week off, go to Philadelphia, and get married.

The honeymoon route back to Buffalo was planned

so that they could visit towns with tire shops, peeking in the windows. It was always nice to know what the out-of-town tire men were doing.

And so we Greenbaum children were to grow up as Buffalonians, speaking in flat midwestern accents, trudging through endless dark and windy winters. Had Daddy been interested in becoming a candy man working for Grandpop, our childhood would have been warmer, and we would have spoken the rounder pronunciations of Philadelphia.

We often complained about living in Buffalo. My father had an answer that was completely satisfactory to him.

"We don't have earthquakes," he'd say.

And besides that, the Chamber of Commerce answered their mail.

Many people worked at Motor Tire Supply Company over the years. There was Henry, who spent his life as manager; Miss Lou Nuermberger, tall and gentle, the best bookkeeper on earth; Howard Nichols, fine mechanic and leading daredevil in the retail tire game.

When I was small, the company had a motorcycle with a sidecar in which Howard and Eddie Ziffle would embark on bill-collecting expeditions. There was some danger in this. A lot of the customers had knives. But Howard gave their presence added zest and force by cutting all left turns so sharply that Eddie, in the sidecar, rose up in the air.

For over forty-five years the store opened at nine and closed at six or ten on alternate evenings. My father never missed a day. He arrived five minutes before opening. Firms along Main Street could set their clocks by the arrival of his Pierce Arrow.

He'd bought this car in nineteen twenty-six. With its

huge headlight eyes growing right out of its fenders and its twenty coats of baked deep green lacquer, our Pierce had a handsome reptile look. It had a beautiful box of tools right on the running board, vases in the back for cut flowers, and little brass stopcocks on the cylinders where you squirted gas to start it in cold weather.

"Now there's a fine piece of machinery." My father would admire it. Then he would sock one of the fenders with a dull thud. "Aluminum!" he would say. The body was made of aluminum, a rare new metal then. As a child I had a notion that they saved enough aluminum foil from chewing gum until they had enough to make a car and that's why they cost so much.

My father really knew how to handle the Pierce. At stop signs he could make it play music by letting the clutch out a bit and shifting partway into gear. To play higher notes, he fed more gas to her. He could play the first part of "Valencia" and "Button Up Your Overcoat" as far as "when the wind blows" but not as far as "free."

"Are you sure you're not hurting it?" my mother would say.

"You can't hurt a piece of engineering like this transmission," he'd say.

The older we got the fonder he became of that car. And the older the Pierce got, the more ashamed of it Mamma and the girls became. When we passed certain key locales where it was necessary to make an impression, they would slump down so they wouldn't be seen. They went down on Nottingham Terrace and Delaware Avenue, really hitting the floor when we passed Temple Beth Zion.

Each year when the new car models came out, my mother left folders around the house, hoping something modern would catch my father's eye. She always hoped he'd buy a car like the ones she rode in with other ladies to play Mah-Jongg or to the Fort Erie races. He treated these brochures with scorn. I remember the year the streamlined Chrysler came out. My crowd thought it was terrific. My father stared at the folder. "Tin balloon!" he scoffed. He tore it up, throwing it into our gas fireplace among the fake logs and moss.

How nice it would be to be able to say that the Pierce became my first "dating" car, to be able to tell of long moonlit rides along Lake Erie, with my arm around Ralpha Becker or Irene Egbert or even Claire Hochgrebe. But the Pierce left our family before I reached that stage of development.

Like many terrible things happening then, it was because of Hitler. War was closing in on Europe. The price of aluminum soared.

The car was stolen on a Thursday night while my father was having a sweat and rub at the Montefiore Club. The police thought the thief must have followed him for a couple of weeks to learn his habits.

No crime ever precipitated more phone calls. There were calls without letup. Calls to detectives, desk sergeants, judges, and the chief of police.

Just before dawn Friday, an incoming call made it through. The Pierce had been found in the woods, stripped of her aluminum. We hung over the upstairs banister in our pajamas, listening.

"No," my father said quietly, "no, no, I don't want to look at it." He hung up and we all went to bed.

We never really knew for sure, but as long as she lived my mother stuck to her story. She always said she won fifty dollars at the Fort Erie track and gave it to two men to steal the Pierce Arrow.

Just Bring in an Honest Face

The modus operandi of Motor Tire Supply never changed. An area known as "the office" was separated from the store proper by a wood-and-glass partition in which there was an opening. Customers made their weekly payments at this window. Lou or one of the girls would take the payment and ring it up on an enormous register which printed out the whole transaction.

There my father sat behind his huge roll-top desk keeping an eye on everything. Even if he was writing a letter or telephoning he could tell when a customer was wandering around the store not being waited on.

He then did a stylish thing he'd picked up in his travels throughout Ohio, Pennsylvania, and New York. It came from his taking in the way a hotel desk clerk would shout "Front!" when a bellboy was needed.

My father would bark out, "Henry, Front!" Henry would appear from the rear of the store to work his charms. Soon the visitor was in hock for four Kelly Springfields and a spare.

The business had a special sound of its own. It was located right under a roller rink. All day long you heard the eternal rise and fall of skates rumbling around the oval, like surf breaking. Every few minutes a loud, sour organ would moan out a Strauss waltz... especially the "Blue Danube," which I still loathe.

Most of the customers were reliable. They made their one- or two-dollar payments every week to keep their credit ratings good. But there was one customer who arrived drunk to make his payment every Saturday. He always hid the payment money from himself in his shoe so he wouldn't spend it on liquor. My father called him the "shikker."

One Saturday morning the "shikker" arrived, weaving and shouting and waving a tire with a bruise on it. My father happened to be out in the store, having watched Henry and Howard prepare a window display. The boys had gone to wash up. The "shikker" held up his tire, demanding a new one.

My father examined it with expertise. The "Blue Danube" played upstairs, the ceiling rumbled.

"Now, what we have here is a curb bruise. You run head-on into a curb. I'm afraid the warranty don't signify on that."

"New tire!" the "shikker" said. "You damn Yid!"

"Now let me understand this..." my father began. The "shikker" threw a half-nelson on him, sending the tire into the bicycle department. Although small, my fa-

ther was a good fighter. But the fellow had him pinned and was working a penknife open with his free hand.
The skates rumbled.
The "Blue Danube" wailed.
"Henry, Front!" my father said.
Henry came out and saved his life.

As Motor Tire Supply grew, my grateful father decided to do something for humanity. He would open a school where he would teach the selling of tires on credit.
He composed an ad for the tiremen's journal. Having always been impressed by a certain World War One recruiting poster, he adopted its theme. There he was in high starched collar and black moustache, twenty-nine years old, pointing and saying: "Alexander Greenbaum will train you in credit tire retailing!"
A man from Cincinnati answered the ad. He was the only one. He came to Buffalo and, as he was broke, lived in the store. They called him "the student."
The student slept in the basement. He took most of his meals at the Chinese restaurant across the street.
He listened and learned. After six months, he went back to Cincinnati and opened a tire store. He never made a major move without first writing to my father. He prospered.
It goes to show. People can see opportunity pointing right at them and only one in thousands will take advantage of it.
For a few years, while I was very young, there were two stores. The second store was run by Uncle Morris, who wasn't really an uncle. He had been in vaudeville and was a bachelor around Buffalo. As a child, he had been one of Gus Edwards's vaudeville "newsboys," along with Walter Winchell and Eddie Cantor and George Jessel. He could dance and sing. His speaking

voice was a straight man's gravelly stage voice. He knew every song ever written, always had on a new suit, drove a convertible, and kept plenty of candy around in brown bags.

My father had no sense of humor. He thought Al Jolson was funny. But funny people stuck by him. Mamma was funny, and so were Henry and Uncle Morris.

Uncle Morris married Teddy, a bleached blonde, all white teeth, lipstick, and perfume, who was associated with the chorus in some way. She was the perfect *shiksa*. The Bureau of Standards in Washington could have used her to define what *shiksa* meant. I was mad about her. My father said that she was Morris's wife and that was that.

Now Uncle Morris really needed to settle down. He had responsibilities and couldn't walk around Buffalo doing the waltz clog and telling jokes. So they opened another store on Main Street for Uncle Morris. The idea was that people seeing these two stores just across the street from each other would think they were in terrific competition, killing themselves to give the public bargains.

But they needed a name.

And they thought of a good one: Montgomery Ward.

Not too Jewish-sounding. Had a good familiar ring about it. A fine name.

"Montgomery Ward" ran along pretty well. The big problem was Uncle Morris. Every time he came across Main Street to tell my father something, he'd get happy about being outdoors, do a dance step, and get hit by a car. My father begged him to phone in his questions before every bone in his body was broken.

Uncle Morris's store did business right up until the other Montgomery Ward got its lawyers into action.

I was sort of pleased to see Uncle Morris released

from the store. He belonged out. My father said that Morris had become a "luftmensh," living on air. Morris and Teddy became my heroes, driving all over the country with the top down, coming back to Buffalo to thrill us with stories of faraway places.

I was always small for my age and hated my smallness. Every time Teddy came back to town she would say the wrong thing. After a winter at the races in Florida, she would say, "Well, honey, you ought to become a jockey. You'd be a darling jockey and it don't look like you're ever going to grow another inch."

After a visit to Southern California, where Teddy'd gone movie crazy, she said, "Honey, you could be another Mickey Rooney any time. You're lots smaller than he is!"

I was at the height of adolescent acne and shyness when I was put to work in the store Saturdays and summers. This was partly to learn the business and partly for calling my sister, Doris, "great big bitch."

I was frightened of the customers and spent long days hiding in stacks of tires. It was finally decided that I would help Tillie Margolis with the filing cabinet upstairs.

This was a mistake.

It was a mistake because my glands were just about to burst into manhood. The very nearness of Tillie charged me with animal lust. She was about twenty, wore horn-rimmed reading glasses attached to a ribbon around her neck, and said "Thank you, no" instead of "No, thank you." She was real class.

And as people used to say in Buffalo, "She had a nice built on her."

She wore tight skirts that would grow tighter when she stooped to the SKI to ZSK file, which happened often, most of the customers being Polish.

One hot summer day my father had run over to Delaware Avenue to his club. The stench of tires had me dizzy. Tillie was stooping and smiling. Overhead, in Scott's Roller Rink, the floor was rumbling. The "Blue Danube" moaned. In a moment of hormonal madness, it seemed desperately important to kiss her.

"Tillie," I said. My voice cracked, and when she turned, my hot, grasping fingers stabbed her behind the ear. We both heard a terrible crash out in the store.

A leg was hanging down from the middle of the ceiling. It was a leg with a skate on it, all four wheels buzzing. One of the skaters had broken through.

I never kissed Tillie. And I was never anything but a failure at anything else in the store. As my father said sadly, "The boy just ain't a merchandiser."

Uncle Morris died right after World War Two. He was run over in California, coming out of a musical.

When Al Greenbaum died many years later, he was in the act of scribbling percentages, mark-ups, and ideas for ads in a notebook.

The Candy King

It is said that my mother's father, Dovid Seltzer, sailing by steerage from Russia at seventeen, had this conversation with a wise old *landsman* he'd met on the crowded decks.

Grandpop: "Tell me, sir, what is a good name for a man to have in America?"

Landsman: "My boy, the best name you can have in America is Goldberg."

Grandpop became David Goldenberg, the Candy King. To this day, Goldenberg's Peanut Chews are a standard candy product in the Northeast. In the beginning, Grandpop made candy that he sold from a tray on the streets of Philadelphia. He married Grandma, a personable girl from Rumania; the tray became a store; two boys arrived, then my mother, Rose, and four more girls.

At first, they lived in a tenement on Frankfort Avenue, which they shared with the family of Leopold, the hatmaker. When Mamma was a baby, she tried to swallow a bar of Fels Naphtha soap. Grandmother Leopold picked her up by the feet and shook it out.

One of the Leopold boys, Isadore Edwin, was stage-struck. As a teen-ager, he began working out comedy routines with hats from his father's shop. Eventually he was to become known as Ed Wynn. As Grandma used to say, "Isadore became a very nice star." I thought him screamingly funny. The two heroes of my childhood were Ed Wynn and Lindbergh.

The Goldenbergs worked hard and were soon able to move from Frankfort Avenue to North Broad Street. Among Grandpop's creations were the "Poppa Lik" sucker, the "After-Dinner Mint," the term "Salt Water Taffy," and, of course, the classic "Goldenberg's Peanut Chew," which was to Goldenberg what the Model T was to Ford.

David Goldenberg was the American Dream come true. A beloved captain of industry: round, freckled, bald, and white-moustached, with sparkling blue eyes, he was a living Jewish Santa Claus. When I was small, he loved to hear me tell jokes. The reward for a good joke was an avalanche of laughter, hugs, and kisses. I can still remember one of my biggest hits.

Me: "Grandpop, ask me how is my father."

Grandpop (heavy Russian accent): "Okay, I'm asking. How is your father?"

Me: "He's a nudist."

The Candy King

Grandpop (starting to lose control): "Yee. Yee. A nudist?"

Me: "Yes, when I come home late, he says, 'Nu, dis is a fine time to come home.'" On that one, he almost fell out of a sailboat off the New Jersey shore.

Even though we lived in Buffalo, my parents always referred to Philadelphia as "home." Relatives shuttled between the two cities. Grandpop and Grandma were visiting us in the late twenties when the "Peace Bridge" to Canada opened. It replaced the slow ferryboat which in summer allowed swarms of flies, called "Canadian Flies," to settle over the car. On the Canadian side, equally dense clouds of insects designated as "American Flies" descended. They were all the same flies. Now one could drive at forty miles an hour across the Niagara River. No more flies. No more cries from Mamma at each lurch of the ferry, "Al, we're sinking!"

Returning from Canada, our Pierce Arrow crossed the bridge's midpoint. Everyone shouted, "Now we're in Canada . . . now we're in the United States!" My father turned to the rear seats. "Listen, Pop, these American customs birds are real *momzers*. So let me answer for you and Grandma. If they hear an accent, we're in hot water." They agreed.

When we reached the customs kiosk, the following ensued.

Customs (to Father): "Where were you born, sir?"
Father: "Philadelphia."
Customs (to Mamma): "And you, madam?"
Mamma: "Philadelphia."
Customs (to children): "Born?"
Children: "Buffalo." "Buffalo." "Buffalo."
Customs (to Grandma): "And you, madam, where were you born?"

Father: "She was born in . . ."
Grandma (in her Rumanian accent, classy, but not foreign): "Pheeledelpheeahh."
Customs (to Grandpop): "You, sir?"
Grandpop (jealous of Grandma): "NEV YOR-RUCK!"
They kept us for two hours.

It was Grandpop's custom, after a day at the factory, to relax in his huge chair, practicing gear shifting for his driving test, dreaming up new candy inventions, and listening to the radio. He adored "Amos 'n' Andy," and enjoyed "The Rudy Vallee Show," which followed it on Thursdays. One night he said to Uncle Dan, "Dan, I'm thinking about this Rudy. Maybe we should try a new item, 'The Rudy Vallee Bar.' "

The next morning, Grandpop dictated a letter. "Rudy," he said, "we'd like to do you in Brazil nuts with shredded coconut on a caramel base; chocolate covered." For a fee, the crooner consented.

"The Rudy Vallee Bar" came on the market, but no one seemed to like it. It even received the candy game Kiss of Death . . . none of the salesmen ate their samples. Uncles Arthur, Harry, and Dan persuaded Grandpop to drop the product.

One evening shortly thereafter, Grandpop was in his chair, shifting gears and listening to "Amos 'n' Andy." Then Rudy Vallee came on, singing his famous theme, "My time is your time. Your time is my time . . ."

Grandpop jumped up, cutting the radio off. "Not on my radio, you son of a bitch," he said.

Ironically, the Candy King had diabetes. Friday evenings, when the clan gathered, it was hard for him to resist certain tempting dishes. Womenfolk watched him carefully, often in vain. "Let me just take a little look at those pickles," he'd suggest, devouring them.

Each summer, he rented a house in Ventnor, New Jersey, a tremendous Victorian affair with twin verandas encircling its two stories. It was just off the Atlantic City boardwalk, a block from the Elephant Hotel, a residence not for elephants but built to look like one. People rented rooms there.

For me, the weeks in Ventnor were absolute enchantment. There were swimming and sand and snow cones and catching starfish and, best of all, autogyros pulling bright banners along the coast. Nothing in life interested me more than aviation. And spectacular thrills beyond description were in the offing. They began one evening on our after-dinner boardwalk stroll.

Families sauntered along, some transported in wicker carriages pushed by black men in straw hats. The night air was soft, flavored with Atlantic City smells: the sea, candy and cooking food, perfume and Noxzema.

A trembling in the sky. At first, few people noticed. Then it grew louder. "Zeppelin!" someone said. Then, others took it up. "Zeppelin! Zeppelin!"

It came from the sea, appearing to be a low cloud. Then, as it drew closer, searchlights threw shafts of white light up against the machine's silver belly. Soon it was directly overhead, filling the sky, filling the ears, fearsome, thrilling, massive throbbing engines pulsing the pit of the stomach.

Grandpop explained that the craft was the *Los Angeles*, probably heading for the new naval airship base in Lakehurst. Each summer after that, we saw several dirigibles ... each experience awesome.

The summer I was fifteen, things went wrong. Grandpop's diabetes took on devious complications. He spent many days in his room. At the same time, Grandma decided that the maids were trying to poison her. She refused all food except hard-boiled eggs, which she peeled herself, saying, "I eat everything except the shells from eggs." A diminutive, charming woman, she would be afflicted by mild paranoia for the rest of her long life. It was devastating to Grandpop. Increasingly he'd announce, "I'm not so hot this morning," and stay in bed. He had trouble breathing, lost his appetite, and his regular Philadelphia doctor drove to Ventnor in a black Franklin. Early in August, to our surprise and grief, he died in the house at the shore. No sooner had they taken him away than the place filled with adult relatives from Philly and Jersey towns and Buffalo. Grandpop, never willing to discuss death, especially his own, had left no will. Through the following nights, arguments echoed upward to the second and third floors where the children were supposed to be sleeping. They debated who had married into the family and who had been born into it, who had worked in the factory and who hadn't. Voices were raised, and women cried. Usually they were calmed by my father's strong, reasonable voice.

After that summer, there was no more Atlantic City for us. But we still got to Philadelphia, usually by Pullman, for Christmas. We remained close to the family, especially Grandma. One summer, while visiting us in Buffalo, she said to Mamma, "Rose, dear, I want you should burn my white shoes!"

"Why?"

"I'm telling you why, Rose. Because the refugees put microphones in them, and they're talking."

"Now, Ma, that's silly. It's a beautiful day. Take some stale bread out on the lawn and feed the birds." Grandma agreed. But, in five minutes, she ran back into the house.

"Rose, burn the shoes! Right away! Quick!"

"Ye gods! What now?"

"I was feeding the birds. I said, 'Come on, little birdies, give Grandma a kiss,' and the white shoes said, 'Kiss my ass!' "

Following the war, after Mamma died, I was living frugally in Greenwich Village. Cousin Jules stayed overnight with me. He returned to Philadelphia with the news that Everett was starving to death in New York. Grandma, Aunt Leah, Aunt Florence, and Aunt Edie were about to depart for an apartment they'd rented in Hollywood Beach, Florida. They decided that I'd drive them down. Then, for two weeks, they'd feed me until I "looked like a person." The plan had a sensible ring to it. I took the train to Philly.

As a change from my grimy Manhattan existence, driving Aunt Leah's big Buick south was splendid.

So far, the journey had been enjoyable. The aunts chatted. In the back seat, Grandma was busy with her latest eccentricity: guarding a black cloth in which were wrapped "the possessions." Aunt Florence confided that she'd peeked at "the possessions" during the night. The inventory listed several broken watch bands, assorted paper clips, and chicken bones.

I had pulled out to pass a bus when Aunt Leah stamped on nonexistent brakes. "Too close! ... No more passing!"

"Now, Aunt Leah," I said, "I'm really an excellent driver. After all, in the service, they trusted me to lead a formation of eighty-five planes. Any more criticism of my driving and I'll mash the gas pedal to the floor." Brash, but effective ... for two days.

We were just outside of Jacksonville when I pulled out to pass. Aunt Leah stiffened. "Look out for that truck!"

Grandma, hunched over her black bundle, called from the back seat, "Step on it, Ev!"

In the Goldenberg family, I was the benedict, not marrying until the age of thirty-six. I took my young bride east for introductions. Grandma, then in her nineties, was living in an attractive nursing home. She looked at me, not a glimmer of recognition in her eyes. Then, suddenly, she became lively.

Turning to my wife, she cocked her head toward me. "That's Rose's boy," she said.

Taking Off

In a world sharply divided between Jew and Gentile, my father assigned proper activities to both sides. Soldiers, sailors, police, and flagpole sitters were Gentile. Wedding-ring salesmen were Jewish. Automobile dealers were Gentile.

All hunters, fishermen, and hikers were Gentile. He summed this up one day when we were caught in traffic behind a camper. "I'll never understand," he said, "why the *Goyim* want to sleep in the woods."

But the most dangerous, foolhardy, and Gentile occupation of all was flying.

And from boyhood, it was my passion. When I was

nine, I experienced an event tantamount to a miracle.

I flew.

One Sunday after lunch, my father had driven the girls and me down Genesee Street for the papers. Then, instead of going home, he guided the Pierce out of town, past the stores, past the Polish Cemetery, past the last bowling alley, to Cheektowaga. And there in a field, the spring sun warming their red and yellow slablike wings, were airplanes at rest. A biplane landed. Passengers climbed out, laughing, waving to their friends. It was Sunday afternoon at Becker's Airport.

I have often tried to explain Daddy's behavior that day. But suffice it to say that the depression hadn't hit him yet, the weather was fair, he had a good cigar, and I hadn't pinched either of my sisters, Doris or Sylvia, in two hours.

"What the deuce!" he said. "We may as well get it out of your system for once and all. If we live through it, it'll be worthwhile."

In a moment, *mirabile dictu,* the two of us were being strapped into the front cockpit of an OX5 Eaglerock biplane.

There were shouts of "switch on" and "throttle cracked" and "contact"; shouts which stirred my blood as "Mark Twain!," "Let go the buoy!," and "Starboard lead there!" must have thrilled a dock kid on the Mississippi a century before.

Someone gave the heavy wooden propeller a tug. The engine exploded into life, turning the propeller so fast it blurred to a disk. But you could feel it pulling us over the rough sod into the air. This manmade bird of dope and leather and gasoline lifted us up out of dingy old Buffalo, turning the city into a fresh-painted toy town on a glass lake.

Wanting to savor the experience to the hilt, I slipped out from beneath the belt to stand on the seat. The wind whipped my hair and flopped my mouth open. I laughed like a hyena. Daddy's strong hands clutched my ankles until the pretty wire wheels of the Eaglerock settled back into the brown grass. It was over.

We were helped to the ground. "We must look like a couple of first-class cuckoos," my father said as we returned to our loved ones. "But if we got this *mishegass* out of your system it's worthwhile."

He was counting on me to work in the tire store or, if I really turned out bad, to be a doctor.

He didn't know he was talking to a boy who said goodnight to a rotogravure picture of Lindbergh every night, a boy who dissolved celluloid combs in acetone to make model-airplane glue. He didn't know he was talking to a boy who had just returned from the finest prepuberty ten minutes on record in Erie County.

Airplanes remained my religion.

In my early teens I found that I could get to Becker's Airport on my bike, spend a couple of hours, and return home in time for dinner. The owner of Becker's was a stocky, red-faced, tough Irishman named Jack Drescher. Jack understood the heart of a plane-crazy kid who clung to the fence watching takeoffs and landings, listening to the sweet sounds of clanking, oil-throwing, radial engines.

After he had seen me a few times, he let me hang around inside the fence. In a little while, I fell into a time-honored ritual of sky-struck boys. I was allowed to wash planes in return for delicious moments in the air.

If I was able to get out to Becker's on a Sunday afternoon, Jack let me fly with him as he stunted to attract crowds. I had complete faith in him and the airplane. It never occurred to me that we might hit the high-tension wires we skimmed or fail to flip right side up from upside down.

In return I sold ride tickets. My distaste for selling was overcome by the feeling that I was a "barnstormer," one of the romantic characters who hopped from town to town taking farmers up for a penny a pound. Daddy never chastised me for all of this. Never scolded, never criticized. He was perfectly calm and reasonable. He never knew about it.

At the age of seventeen I found myself out of high school fighting for my life, i.e., a life outside the tire store. All of the things I loved were considered frivolous time wasters: machines, music, the theater, movies, and, of course, airplanes.

I had managed to rebuild two wrecked motorcycles and use them for transportation to high school. With this concrete evidence, I convinced Daddy that I could become an engineer. There were several members of his club who were engineers. They made a comfortable living. One of them was even called "Doctor." Everybody knew he wasn't a real doctor. He was an electricity doctor.

I went to Boston to attend M.I.T. . . . certainly not the best place in the world for me, but far from the sulfurous stacks of Kelly Springfield tires waiting to swallow me up in Buffalo. Each week I received twenty dollars from home. It went for rent, food, second-balcony theater seats, and flying lessons at the East Boston Airport.

My scholastic record at the Massachusetts Institute of Technology was phenomenal. I was able to keep my average grade one-hundredth of a point above 2.00 for three years. The critical number was 2.00. When you sank to that, they threw you out.

I now knew about two areas of life where I didn't belong: tire stores and engineering laboratories. But I was in wonderful Boston, where I lived for moments in second balconies and cockpits of Fleet Biplanes.

At the end of my third year (my second as a sophomore), I hit 2.00. Suddenly, and ahead of schedule, I was out of college.

The world was not waiting with open arms for engineering graduates during the Depression. And certainly not for fellows who flunked out of M.I.T. a year ahead of their classmates, degreeless, not knowing logarithm tables from steam tables, having no use for the slide rules sticking out of their pockets except to impress girls who, in fact, weren't even looking.

It meant goodbye to the culture capital of the East. As I left South Boston Station in the all-night coach train, I could see my reflection gazing back at me from the filthy window. A twenty-year-old failure.

Back home, Daddy welcomed me like a cat licking his chops over a newly arrived mouse. "Wait till you see the store." He smiled. "We've put in a line of Emerson radios."

But, once again, I was able to escape merchandising. I was hired on the night riveting crew at Bell Aircraft.

This end of the aviation world was far from the romance of the blue I had dreamed of. Since it was April, Buffalo was still in the death clutch of winter. Bell was a converted radiator factory north of the city, close to the river. Through snowdrifts and blowing sleet I skidded between home and my riveting shift in a used Model-A Ford that I'd gotten for twenty-five bucks. Every dawn I came home to bed, plucking riveter's cleco fasteners from my pockets, stinking of chromate paste, my ears ringing from the din of five hundred rivet guns.

When the war began in Europe, Civilian Pilots Training Programs were started at various universities, including the University of Buffalo. Two years of college and reasonable health were the only requirements. If you were otherwise employed, you could fly early in the morning and attend ground school at night.

I was accepted in the first group of the C.P.T.P. Bell allowed me to work the day shift. For the first time in my life, I was doing something I loved and which I was able to do better than others.

One crisp morning shortly after flying instruction began, my instructor stepped out of the lovely, kitelike Piper Cub.

"Go ahead," he said, "you don't need me in there."

That morning the sky belonged to me. It was the greatest joy I had ever known. Breathtaking freedom! In the air-ocean a flyer is a fish while the earthbound are crabs scuttling along the bottom.

Soon I finished the primary course and moved on to advanced lessons in acrobatics and cross-country. Here the instructor was my old pal, Jack Drescher. The cloth-covered airplanes we flew then have rarely been excelled in beauty ... Waco Biplanes for stunts, and for cross-country the graceful, birdlike Stinson Reliants.

Within a year, I was a civilian flight instructor teaching primary flying to naval aviation cadets at the University of Maryland. We flew out of a tiny airfield, the College Park Airport. It was America's earliest military field, having as much history as trees surrounding the runway.

In a few months, Pearl Harbor occurred and we were at war. Since one hand of the government doesn't know what the other is doing, my draft notice arrived. They wanted me for a soldier.

I began trying to enlist in air forces: the Army, the Navy, and even the Royal Canadians, driving up to Hamilton, Ontario, for that desperate move. Everywhere I was told that I was too small and too skinny and had hyperforia of the left eye, which meant that it would roll upward if I got low on oxygen.

Before going into the infantry I decided to try the Navy recruiters in New York City. There, the Navy doctors detected the eye and the rotten body in two seconds. But they told me to wait.

I was afraid they'd decided to turn me into a sailor ... someone who stayed in the basement of the ship all day tying knots.

A bored doctor returned.

"We're supposed to keep an eye open for flight instructors," came the perfect news. "You have experience and seven hundred hours. Can you stay in New York for a couple of days while we send to Washington for waivers on your hyperforia and minimal chest expansion?"

How did the man ask such an important question so calmly?

I took a room at the Young Men's Christian Association and followed their instructions ... to eat bananas and cream for two days. When I returned to the dreary recruiting office on Canal Street, I did a lot of stretching to be tall and scrunching down to be heavy. The waivers had arrived from the Pentagon. By lunch time, I was in a small room with a lot of older fellows taking an oath not to lead any revolutions against the U.S.A.

We were officers, classified "Aviation Provisional"; that is, we were officers providing we could get through flight and instructors' schools in three months. I found myself out on the streets of New York in an ensign's uniform, hiding from sailors because I didn't know how to return their salutes.

    Back home in Buffalo, the family couldn't believe that their ne'er-do-well had been given a blue suit with gold stripes on the sleeves. Suddenly I became an object of pride. But the evening I was to depart for Corpus Christi, Texas, Mamma suddenly began to regret the whole thing. She couldn't face coming to see me off. My father drove me down to the train station. Never very tall, he had always walked hunched over. "Dad's looking for money," we used to say. That night he was ramrod straight—the old colonel seeing the junior officer off to battle, a gloved finger held up in farewell.

The Prince of the Yellow Perils

Corpus Christi, a small town of bleached-white buildings and palm trees, vibrated pleasantly to the drone of Navy training planes overhead: formations of silver SNJs, gray PBY flying boats, and clusters of yellow-painted primary trainers, the N3Ns.

About fifty of us lived in the barracks. My classmates had been flying in civilian life, accumulating thousands of hours. Roughhouse Reagan, who reminded me of Jack Drescher, had been instructing in China for Chiang Kai-shek. Whiskey-voiced Berringer had been a movie stunt pilot in Hollywood. The Glasscock brothers, Don and Mike, had been Texas oil playboys who owned their own planes. Jimmie Robinson had been a successful

Memphis businessman and sportsman pilot. Walter Griffith, like me, had come out of the C.P.T.P., but his left eye didn't roll and he was big. He also played cards, drank booze, and was engaged.

My first solo flight in the Navy came very close to disaster. I was tightening my parachute harness when B. J. Berringer came up to me.

"Well, kid. Ah see we gonna solo now."

"Yep!"

"Tell you what. Meet me at five thousand over the Gulf. We'll have ourselves some fun."

Flattered by an invitation from the old pro, a man who had flown Fokkers in *Hell's Angels*, I hastened to accept the invitation.

I took off and threaded my way out of the traffic pattern. Then I climbed up over the shoreline to five thousand. He was there, wagging his wings at me. Berringer did a loop and I did a loop.

Berringer did a slow roll and I did a slow roll.

Berringer did a nice Immelmann turn and so did I.

Berringer did an exhibition-style Immelmann: rolling out straight up.

I did an exhibition-style Immelmann, tucked my feet up under the instrument panel and got the stick stuck forward, but not on purpose.

So this was how you did an inverted spin!

I was hanging out under the plane; couldn't get my feet back on the rudders. My goggles were flopping around, and all kinds of Texas dirt was coming up from under the floorboards, blowing into my eyes.

I went through four thousand feet and then, very quickly, three, and then two. I could see the davits on a fishing boat whirling beneath my head. So this was it! I was going to die on my first solo flight in the military ... still a virgin.

The Prince of the Yellow Perils

Maybe there was time to jump. I groped for the safety belt release, but my fingers slipped away from it. Then I noticed the throttle was wide open. I closed it. Suddenly, I was no longer spinning, but still upside down. I brought the stick back, pulling out just over the beach.

Berringer led me home ... all the way to parking. I climbed out, legs rubbery.

"Know what ya done there, kid?" Berringer rasped. "Three inverted spins. Progressive. Right smack out of one into the other. I followed ya all the way down."

I thanked him for a swell time and went to lie down.

Even though the fatality rate for Corpus averaged one a day, we passed through Primary and Basic without incident. Now, all we had to do to win our wings was to finish Instructors' School in New Orleans.

But ours, the first class to go through the new school, was badly organized, and the course ended in tragic confusion. During night flying, two groups were given conflicting runway assignments. Four Stearmans ran into each other head-on. Three officers perished in the crash, two of them decapitated. One lived, badly burned. For days, I couldn't shake the sound and the sight and the smell of the accident.

Except for the fellows in the crash, all of my group finished the course. Graduation day was warm enough for white uniforms.

Alphabetically just ahead of Walter Griffith, I stepped up to the skipper to have my wings pinned on and receive a large scroll ... "*know all men by these presents that [skinny] Ensign Greenbaum, U.S.N.R. [with the rolling eye], has completed the prescribed course of training and, having met successfully the requirements of the course, has been designated NAVAL AVIATOR....*"

We went into town for another ceremony. Walter married Myrtie, his girl from Syracuse. I was best man.

After the wedding, I strolled down the main stairway of the hotel, catching my reflection in the mirror paneling.

I looked wonderful! Heroic and possibly handsome.

I entered the bar. Soft music mingled with the hum of early evening chatter. The dapper black bartender looked up from the glass he was polishing, took a look at me, and called out . . .

"The Prince is here!"

I ordered what I then considered to be a very worldly drink—a gin rickey—and drank it in a worldly way, though it burned my throat.

Then, tipping the bartender fifteen cents, I ambled into the lobby. A woman approached me, extending her hand. This, surely, was someone who had found me irresistible.

"Here, boy," she said, extending a key, "you run right on up to 307 and bring the bags down to the taxi."

Majuro

Pan American Airways' flying boat, the China Clipper, flicked in and out of cloud, flashing over patches of blue sea. White-jacketed stewards served steak-and-egg breakfasts to the passengers: three admirals, four generals, five congressmen, and a juvenile Lieutenant Junior Grade of possible Hebraic origin—me.

Through an administrative bungle in the San Francisco Office of Naval Transportation, I'd been sent to Hawaii on the China Clipper, the last lucky break in what had been, for me, a wonderful war.

For three joyous years, I'd been a flying instructor at the Naval Air Station in Peru, Indiana. Roughhouse

Reagan was my squadron commander. We flew open-cockpit Yellow Perils, winter and summer, day and night, turning out hundreds of Navy pilots. I'd become chief check pilot for acrobatics, developing such panache that I was able to take three bites of a Baby Ruth bar while in the throes of the once-dreaded inverted spin.

Since I'd sluffed off my dreary virginity through the hospitality of lusty farm girls, my social life improved. There'd been Dionysian summertime romps—drinking rum Cokes until 4 A.M., skinny-dipping in the Wabash River, and then, at dawn after an hour's sleep, taking off into the fresh Hoosier skies.

In one respect, we'd done our job too well. No more pilots were needed. I'd been sent to the Naval Air Technical Center in Memphis to take a course in Forward Base Engineering. I feared my flying days in the military were over.

The Clipper splashed gently into Pearl Harbor. As we came down the gangplank, we were greeted by native girls playing ukuleles, dancing the hula. On the pier, a man was reading a newspaper, the first page opened toward us. The headline read, "Roosevelt Dead." A cold gray snake wrapped itself around my viscera.

I was assigned to assist the training officer in the aircraft repair facility at Barber's Point, at the southern end of Oahu. There was little work to be done, but, nevertheless, I was imprisoned eight hours a day at a desk. Emotionally triggered to resent my superior, Lieutenant Brantland, I was fortunate: He was truly loathsome. A former high-school principal in Ohio, he'd wangled a lieutenant's commission as an educator. Thin-lipped, pedantic, with rimless glasses and a rimless mouth, he somehow fancied himself an old salt.

"Come aboard, Greenbaum," he'd call over an intercom, when he wanted me to cross the room to his desk. He was full of nautical expressions . . . "bulkhead," "secure," "deck," "eighteen hundred hours."

"I'm a stickler for discipline," he'd say. "I run a tight ship."

On the rare occasions when we engaged in "conversation," he reached new highs in creative bigotry. "I'm so proud that Albert Einstein is Episcopalian," he said.

And, "Greenbaum, you're a decent sort of Jew, but if you were to associate with some of the bad ones, you'd turn rotten in no time at all."

I soon became a sullen lout. Unfortunately, my promotion to full lieutenant came up for consideration. As my superior, Brantland was required to evaluate me in my fitness report.

He showed me what he had written. Tardy reporting to duty: three times. Out of uniform at officers' mess (red socks and moccasins): twice.

Life outside of office hours was not much better. Men outnumbered women five thousand to one. Women became remote, unattainable, almost mythological creatures.

Once, a shipment of enlisted women, WAVEs, arrived from the mainland. Naturally, even the plainest of them became tremendously popular. With great difficulty, I managed to arrange transportation and a date. I had always found girls with overbites tremendously attractive, *vide* Loretta Young and Gene Tierney. But overbite runs into the law of diminishing returns. Too much and a chipmunk effect takes over. The parachute rigger who agreed to spend an evening with me was fat, hirsute, and well into chipmunk. But she was female and I was desperate.

After an evening of forced conversation, I parked our

"car," a six-wheeled weapons carrier, in a sugarcane field and put my arm around her. There were to be no kisses, however.

"Not on the first date," she said.

It struck me that if this had happened to anyone else, I would have thought it hilarious. Since my job involved about an hour of actual work per week, I spent the next four days writing a one-act play about a homely girl becoming instantly popular in wartime Hawaii. I put Brantland into it, and, of course, myself, happily restored to flight duty. In the ship's store, I'd seen a poster announcing that the Author's League in New York was holding a script contest for naval personnel. I mailed the play, *The Arrival of the Female*, to them, and promptly forgot about it.

Two days later, the death knell of my military career tolled across the seas from the Pentagon. I received notice that my promotion had been denied, and I was shipped west.

After days of changing planes and waiting on grease-soaked coral islands, I arrived in a paradise of palms, white beaches, and aquamarine water. This was Majuro Atoll in the Marshalls, where I was to spend the remainder of the war.

Coconut, breadfruit, and banana trees ringed her lagoon. Her reef teemed with fish, and her natives radiated charm. Of all the island bases taken by the Allies in 1944, Majuro was a jewel. The enemy was twenty miles away, on Mille Atoll, and they hadn't attacked in months.

There were three types of habitation. Officers lived in tents mounted over plank floors. Steel Quonset huts served most other purposes. The Japanese had constructed two wooden structures in their fashion: mortise and tenon joints instead of nails. One was our hospital and the other was the house of Captain Grow, U.S.N., the oldest man I had ever seen in the service, an elderly military lion bearing two badges of honor: his Annapolis ring and verdigris-covered wings of prewar design.

The pulse of life on Majuro was erratic. Whenever a ship of the fleet arrived in the lagoon, the island filled momentarily with strangers. Visiting Air Force, Naval, and Marine combat squadrons roosted with us in order to raid Mille and other more distant targets. They remained for a week or two, then departed. As a result, the people I got to know were the fixed company of the air station. Like me, they all seemed to be in a state of disrepute.

Boozer, a delightful Southerner, had flown his F4F fighter off the *Franklin* into the sea. His squadron commander claimed he'd killed his speed by overuse of the rudder. He was sent to Majuro.

His tentmate, Faulkner, had the courage to say he was going to be a poet after the war. He was the only American pilot ever shot down in Texas. In tow-sleeve target practice at Corpus Christi, the plane following him had fired too soon. The bullet went right through Faulkner, but he was able to land before fainting. The shirt he wore that day become his favorite. He wore it as often as possible. It had a hole in the front and a hole in the back. He was sent to Majuro.

Faulkner and Boozer lived in a tent with Faulkner's raccoon. The raccoon bit everybody but Faulkner and Boozer.

Ordinarily, an air station had to have an executive officer. But no aviator of suitable rank was available. Instead, we had a two-and-a-half striper, serving in the position called "first lieutenant." This ground reservist, Lieutenant Commander Sellers, was a former Civil Service employee. A bitter, middle-aged bachelor, he harbored a special hatred for two people he'd never met. They seemed to epitomize everything he missed in life.

"That son of a bitch, Harry James, and that little snip, Betty Grable," he would say. "What do you suppose they're up to right now?" He was sent to Majuro.

Captain Grow, a graduate of the Academy, was old enough to be an admiral. I suspected that his bluntness had not served him well in the politics of the Navy. He was sent to Majuro.

In the next year, conversations between the captain and me were rare and unsatisfying, rather like our first. I tried to launch an explanation of my lack of promotion. After two words, he slammed a fist on his desk.

"Not now, Greenberg! This is not the time for metaphysical discussion. Get yourself on the duty roster down at Air Operations."

From 6 A.M. until noon, I was the Air Operations duty officer. Watching others fly was prolonged torture. Two aircraft were assigned to the station: an SNJ and a Grumman "Duck." They were never flown. Corrosion was setting in. Aluminum turned to white powder. It broke my heart.

Time slowed. Sometimes it seemed that no one remembered we were there. Intermittently, food supplies failed, and we lived on "C" rations. Our principal enemies were starvation and tedium. Most of my shipmates seemed to be able to sublimate the yearning for female companionship with drinking and gambling. Neither interested me. But I found an activity which occupied my mind. I became a student of underwater life.

The reef, an outside ring of coral, was battered by the sea. Great heavings of blue and green water alternately filled and emptied deep caves.

Looking down into the caves through blowholes, one viewed an aquatic circus: always changing, always fascinating.

Huge green parrotfish with viselike crusher jaws munched on the coral itself. Small silver fish ate crumbs from their lips. On the bottom were rocks which turned into living creatures: octopi, orange starfish, fear-inspiring moray eels.

Inside the lagoon, the water was turquoise near the shore, darkening to shades of blue toward the center.

Here I spent long, happy afternoons. The water was warm, swarming with tiny fish of vivid colors. Swimming with snorkel and face mask, I'd quietly work my way into this living kaleidoscope; then, floating weightless, I'd watch for hours.

Through the entire war, I was shot at twice, both occasions the result of foolishness.

As I came off duty one day, a twenty-year-old Air Force pilot invited me to join him on an A-26-C photo reconnaissance mission over Mille. Breaking regulations, I accepted.

The kid was a good host, but a wild pilot. He banked close to the sea, dipping wingtips between breadfruit trees. My concern about his daredevil airwork overshadowed any interest I might have had in the small figures running about Mille with upraised firearms. As we swept between rotting tents, someone seemed to hit the plane with a tackhammer.

Back on Majuro, we found bullet holes along the bottom of the fuselage.

"Twenty-twos," the second lieutenant said. "The poor bastards are running out of supplies."

One night I was awakened by gunshots. A bullet spit

through the canvas of my tent. It was VE Day. The war was over in Europe. Drinking and firing their guns, the Marines were celebrating. One was wounded.

The natives of Majuro had been moved to a remote section of the atoll. Many of the males, however, were recruited to aid us in docking seaplanes. As time went on, a number of them were taught to drive jeeps. They were placid, smiling people who had remained that way despite invasion by missionaries, the Japanese, and us. A gentle people to whom murder, theft, and violence were almost unknown. Their language sounded like running water. The word *"yugliuck"* was a greeting. One soon picked that up, as well as *"inman,"* which meant "good."

One of my first assignments at the airstrip concerned the islanders. Commander Dodge, the Air Operations officer, instructed me that a group of them would be arriving at our junkyard on the seaward end of the airstrip.

"They want some aluminum scrap," he said. "Their leader, Big Mike, won't take anything unless an officer is there. Just give them whatever they want."

I took a jeep to the junkyard and waited. Soon a fleet of outriggers came to shore. *"Yugliuck."* I bowed. *"Inman. Inman."*

They carried a large chair ashore, delighted that I was not only there, but speaking a couple of words of Micronesian. A slender man was carried ashore and placed in the chair. I addressed him.

"Yugliuck, Big Mike," I said. I gestured. "Take anything you want, Big Mike."

For a moment, there was silence. Then . . . laughter. Tears of pleasure ran down their cheeks. I made an embarrassed departure. Dodge said that Big Mike hadn't come with them. The man in the chair was Jehu, the village idiot, whom they always treated with great consideration.

Their humor wasn't always easy to understand. On evenings when we had movies, natives perched in the trees behind our folding chairs. A scene in which a character opened the door of an automobile, got in, and closed the door sent them into gales of hilarity. Ice skating also aroused their risibilities. A Sonja Henie picture all but toppled them from the trees in hysteria.

One afternoon while I was swimming in the lagoon, something tugged at my arm. Thinking I had run into kelp, I tried to shake it off. When a length of the stuff lay across my bare chest, I realized an octopus had attached itself to me.

I began wrestling slippery tentacles. With soft popping of suction cups, they could be pulled off only to be replaced by other slimy appendages. I lost my footing and went under. For a moment, I was able to get my head above water.

"Help!" I hollered.

Someone was in the water with us ... a native work party. They were laughing, holding me up. With easy nonchalance, one of them raised the body of the devilfish so that another could bite into its underside.

As life ran out of my tormentor, it released me. Clouds of black dye swirled through the water.

I had given the Marshallese an entree for their favorite meal. They had given me life. "*Yugliuck*," I said. "*Inman.*"

A letter from home was on my bed. Mamma said she had gone into the hospital for minor surgery. I wasn't to worry. She went on to say that an advertisement had come in the mail. They'd thrown it in the garbage. The garbageman brought it back into the house. It was a five-hundred-dollar war bond.

The one-act play I'd written while trapped behind a desk in Hawaii had won third prize in the Author's League Navy Show Contest. I resolved that if I should contrive to emerge from the war without being shot or eaten, I'd try to become a writer.

One evening in August, I was in communications listening to the midnight news from Melbourne, Australia. Something called the "atomic bomb" had been dropped on Hiroshima. I remembered a lecture I'd heard at M.I.T. on the possibilities of unleashing the power of the atom, and wished I'd paid closer attention.

The pace of events began to accelerate in a very un-Majurolike way.

The next day, a landing craft pulled into the lagoon, carrying a platoon of Marines. They had Japanese prisoners with them. An hour later, another LST came in with more prisoners. Captain Grow was nowhere to be seen. To add to the mystery, a destroyer escort had been ordered to Mille Lagoon.

Around three in the afternoon, the news came out ... the first formal surrender of Japanese territory. Captain Masanori Shiga had handed Mille over to Captain Grow, aboard the destroyer escort, U.S.S. *Levy*.

Even in this barren outpost, there were spoils of war. Everyone received booty. I was given a Samurai sword, a pistol, and a ceremonial dagger.

At lunch the next day, we were joined in the officers' mess by two newcomers, Captain Shiga and his executive officer. They sat straight-backed, showing no emotion. Outside, a Marine guard stood with his rifle.

Majuro

"Talk to them," I said to our translator. "This tension is ruining my digestion."

He did. He spoke to the executive officer. One could see the man warming to his subject. He seemed to describe a tennis game.

"My God," the translator said.

"What?"

"He says he personally beheaded the Corsair pilot who crash-landed on Mille. He says we owe him a debt of gratitude because he did it in one stroke."

Later, someone knocked against the pole of my tent. It was Captain Grow's yeoman.

"Mr. Greenbaum, the captain says Captain Shiga likes your tent. How soon can you secure so that he can move in?"

What was this, the International Brotherhood of Captains? "I'm not moving for the enemy."

In ten minutes, Sellers appeared.

"Now, come on, Greenbaum. Be reasonable."

"They beheaded one of our guys. Is the captain crazy?"

"Better move, if you know what's good for you."

"Watch out, Mr. Sellers. I'll write a letter to Drew Pearson."

"Who's that?"

"Oh, God."

"Please, Greenbaum, he'll have my ass."

I moved. The next morning, I couldn't find my toenail scissors. Going to my tent, I was greeted by the Marine guard.

"Sir?"

"Oh, Corporal, I forgot something in my tent."

"Sir . . . I've been wondering. The prisoner looks . . . uh . . . funny."

We moved closer. Shiga was on the floor, rigid, purple, and belly up. With my toenail scissors, he'd made a ritual hara-kiri scratch on his abdomen. He'd taken cyanide. At the time he was dining with us, he'd had three capsules hidden on him.

Japan surrendered. The war was over. The older officers were sent home. Suddenly, I became Air Operations officer, third in command of the base, an unwanted honor. I wanted to join the others who were beginning their new lives in civilization. My mother was back in the hospital again. I longed to see her.

For several days, Operations ran smoothly, giving me some confidence. Machinist's Mate Vroom visited me. He was about twenty, fun-loving and good company. Like me, he'd always had an eye on the two planes we "owned."

"Say, Mr. Greenbaum, I couldn't get the Duck started, but the SNJ fires up. Can't retract the gear ... all corroded. But I think she'll fly."

Of course! I was in charge. I could get back into the air.

"Now, wait a minute, Vroom. We don't want the old man to see us. Suppose we take off, fly down the strip, and land at the end? We'll never get higher than the trees."

"I'll do a little work on the engine. Close up a couple of induction leaks." He clapped his hands in anticipation. We scheduled the first flight for the next morning.

Word traveled fast. The coming event became known as "The Greenbaum and Vroom Expedition to the Moon."

A surprising number of people turned out to witness our takeoff. Vroom started the engine; a nice, throaty sound. We donned orange rubber flotation jackets. I climbed into the front cockpit; Vroom in back. Releasing the parking brakes, I taxied the machine into position on the downwind end of the runway. I ran up the engine. The magnetos both worked, but the propeller wouldn't come out of flat pitch.

No matter. It was power we wanted, not speed. A fresh blue sea wind spanked right down the coral strip against our nose. We were ready.

For the first time in a year, I pressed a throttle to the stop, feeling the familiar pressure of acceleration against my back.

We were in the air almost instantly. The crowd cheered, waving. Vroom yelped with joy.

In a moment, we were climbing above treetop level. Flying higher would make us visible from the other end of the island. But pushing down, we picked up speed. If I didn't cut the power, we'd overshoot. Now . . . !

For an instant, we settled toward the ground. Did I still remember how to land?

Perfect! Great adventure! We taxied back for another flight. This time, we stayed up longer, ending ten feet from the end of the runway.

"More!" everyone shouted. "Again!"

Chief Petty Officer Daly began taking bets. Odds were made on how close we could come to the water without actually going in. Someone ran for a yardstick.

Naturally, I was carried away. On the third hop, I decided to give them a thrill. I planned on staying up a little too long, pancaking down, and grouploping at the water's edge.

Miscalculation! I held the left brake, starting a left groundloop, but the right wheel hit the shallows. For a dreadful moment, the tail rose, the propeller biting into water. I pulled the mixture; the tail settled.

Silence. No great harm done. The surf tumbled in, rattling stones and shells against the landing gear. Softly, the cooling engine ticked. The gyros slowed, humming sweetly.

"Get out!" someone said. "Get out of that airplane." Sellers, Second in Command and Chief Betty Grable Hater, was standing on the seat of his jeep so that I could see him over the nose.

"How dare you risk the life of an innocent enlisted man! I'm putting you on report."

The Greenbaum and Vroom Expedition to the Moon was over.

Disciplinary action was taken against me in true Naval officer tradition ... I was confined to quarters. Meals were brought on a tray. Visits to latrine or shower were supervised by a Marine bearing arms.

I spent most of my first day of confinement lying on my bunk, reading an old paperback of *David Copperfield*.

After dinner, Faulkner, Boozer, and Vroom came over, bringing Cokes and a radio. We enjoyed a broadcast from Australia, featuring the talents of a young woman who played the trombone.

Vroom had connections in the galley. Around ten-thirty, we built a fire on the beach behind my tent and roasted Vienna sausages.

By eleven, Sellers had reported our activities to the captain. By midnight, my punishment was canceled. I was enjoying it too much.

Many years later, I would write of this as happening during the Korean war to Hawkeye Pierce, the protagonist of a TV show called "M*A*S*H."

Several more months dragged by.

Before dawn one morning, the phone in my tent rang. It was the tower operator. There'd been a bad crash. I raced to the strip.

Majuro

A twin-engine Curtiss transport had taken off carrying the American Military Olympic swimming teams. They'd lost an engine, crashing seven miles off the airstrip. The water at that point was seven miles deep.

The tower operator had done well. He'd notified the destroyer escort, which was underway, and recalled two departing transport planes back to Majuro.

But the D.E. couldn't reach the crash for an hour. From the air, men could be seen swimming desperately, heading in no particular direction.

I remembered that we had fifty life rafts in storage. We loaded them onto the transports. Within a few minutes, they were dropped on the swimmers. Except for exposure and high-octane gasoline skin burns, the Olympic teams survived. Thirty-three men. The cockpit of the Curtiss had broken off on impact, carrying the crew with it into the deep water.

Captain Grow was awarded the Bronze Star for the rescue. At long last, I was promoted and sent home. But some victories aren't worth the winning. Mamma found her last strength to meet me at the train. Then, after just three weeks, she died.

Making
the Rounds

While other veterans were doing sensible things like studying dry cleaning under the G.I. Bill, I decided to storm Gotham ... the Big Apple ... Manhatto-by-the-sea.

Nine hours out of Buffalo, covered with the heavy grime of the Empire State Limited, glutted with train-bought cheese sandwiches on puttylike white bread, I arrived at Grand Central.

One would like to say that he took the express elevator to the top of the Empire State Building and, kicking aside a bit of King Kong spore, shouted out over the city ... "I'll lick you yet, Big Town!"

In actual fact I dragged myself off the train frightened and depressed. After a confused journey by bus and subway, under the impression that I was in Greenwich Village, I rented a room on the Lower East Side where things bit your ankles while you were asleep.

Whatever, you may ask, encouraged me to leave the comfort of my father's home in Buffalo to hurl myself against the bastions of Broadway? Easy money! After all, I'd won a five-hundred-dollar war bond in the Author's League Navy Show Contest. Big dough and short hours. Nothing for it but to go to New York and get into show business.

Which brought me to Avenue B, off Houston Street, scratching my ankles.

I didn't worry about money at first, having saved some in the service. In the forties in New York, it was possible to live on very little. Bus and subway fare was a nickel. A phone call was a nickel. A room was five dollars a week. You could eat on a dollar a day, especially if one of the meals was a tremendous plate of stewed tomatoes, fifteen cents at the Automat.

But how to get into show business? I soon discovered a little publication sold in Times Square called *Actors' Cues*. It told you where there were jobs to be had. Sometimes they were just rumors blown into facts, sometimes out-and-out lies, but once in a while it published real leads that made the false ones worthwhile. At the very least, it provided a war plan for the day. It got you up and going, even if to the wrong places.

I joined a dramatic society, Sunday Theater, which met in a rented hall on Riverside Drive. To remain in Sunday Theater you had to pay two dollars each week by Tuesday. The director rehearsed us over and over in a mystery play which had one great virtue ... many,

many characters. All I remember about it is that people constantly hid behind nonexistent doors, leaping out on cue.

One day in the tenth week, the director arrived with good news. We were soon to do our play for the Du-Mont TV station. We began paying our Tuesday dues and hiding behind the doors with renewed zeal.

On a Wednesday, the director of Sunday Theater disappeared with the funds.

Then there was another institution called the Comedy Writers Workshop. We paid fifty cents each Friday night to hear a discussion of comedy writing. It was promised that a very successful writer for Fred Allen would soon show up to answer questions.

Sure enough, one night he did. He was wearing a camel's hair wraparound overcoat with wide lapels and a white-on-white shirt. Mr. Success. Mr. Broadway.

"How did you do it?" we asked. "How did you get started?"

"Prayer," he replied.

By the end of my first year, I had made a discovery. There was no reason to fear making a fool of yourself. There were so many people coming and going that no matter how gauche you were, you were completely forgotten in a few days. This gave me the nerve of a bandit.

I bluffed my way into tryouts for a small part in the original company of *Mr. Roberts*. Everything was going fine. I hadn't been asked to recite or sing or dance or any of those other things I couldn't do. I had been picked from two hundred fellows ... then fifty ... and finally down to twenty....

Lined up on the stage, we awaited the continuation of the winnowing process. Suddenly we were asked to strip to the waist.

I stood out like an off-white xylophone . . . pale, freckled, ribs sticking out . . . 118 pounds of *chutzpah*.

"You in the center, thank you very much."

"But I'm the only one who isn't holding his stomach in," I protested.

"Thank you. Good day."

It wasn't all struggle and humiliation. There were long, wonderful days at the Museum of Modern Art. And balcony seats or standing room for shows. And meeting people.

One of my neighbors on the East Side was a brilliant, popeyed little black kid named James Baldwin. He was a neighborhood celebrity, having actually been paid thirty-five dollars in cash for writing a book review for the *Trib*.

Jimmie Baldwin took me to my first New York Jewish delicatessen. He introduced me to Kafka, which I understood, Kierkegaard, which I didn't understand, and chocolate egg cream, which I did.

Then there was Cheryl, classical pianist, rich girl, and devotee of the orgone box.

She had become convinced through the teachings of a Dr. Reich that alternate layers of organic and inorganic materials formed a kind of condenser which would trap cosmic energy. If you sat in a phone-boothlike structure made in this way, your health would be improved. In addition, you would become highly charged sexually.

Cheryl's orgone box was her headquarters. It was a deluxe model with special attachments—hat for headaches (or, pulled way down, earaches), gloves for arthritis of the hands, and a variety of plugs for problems in other areas.

Cheryl moved around a lot, always with her box. As she led me through Penn Station on our way to Fire Island, I tried to keep up, balancing the thing on a porter's dolly. "Step on it," she'd say, "we're going to miss the train!"

Sometimes we'd pass other orgone boxes going through the station. Cheryl gave the owners little waves, the way passing MG drivers did in those days.

Getting the box on and off the ferry, Cheryl became Captain Bligh, laying orders on all hands.

When our friendship finally ended, I told her that the trouble with her sex life couldn't be cured by orgones. The trouble was that she was just too bossy.

One day *Actors' Cues* announced a course in TV camera operation at the DuMont studio. This studio was actually located in the center of Wanamaker's Department Store on lower Broadway. Seeing a chance to get in on the ground floor of television, I enrolled.

In no time at all I knew how to focus the picture, dolly in and out, and most important of all, when finished, to remove the huge lens and store it in a blue velvet bag.

The day the course ended, our instructor explained that although we were now qualified to be assistant cameramen, there were no jobs anywhere in town. But he'd be happy to take us to his apartment where we could see our first actual broadcast on a receiving set.

The picture was small and flickery. A couple were pretending to be a charming husband and wife having an adorable quarrel.

We decided that television would never amount to anything after all.

Pizza was served. I had never seen pizza before and put it down as one of the great inventions of our time.

After almost two years I was broke. I began passing up *Actors' Cues* and buying the *Times* to read the help-wanted ads.

Up in the Bronx, a gentleman named Mr. Sunshine wanted someone with an engineering education to work in his plastic button factory. Mr. Sunshine turned out to be a lovely man who was mad about me. He had no son. In time, the button factory would be mine.

Four hundred miles west, along the shores of Lake Erie, there was another lovely man who needed a son to go into his business—my father.

My father sold tires. Mr. Sunshine sold buttons. My father was in Buffalo, which I hated. Mr. Sunshine was in New York, which I loved. Tires bored me. Plastic buttons bored me. Neither one was anything like show business.

Mr. Sunshine wanted an answer soon.

A miracle happened! A letter from my father reminded me that an allotment from my service pay had put eight hundred dollars' worth of war bonds in his possession for me.

I had heard that one could attend the Sorbonne under the G.I. Bill. I thanked Mr. Sunshine and sailed tourist class on the S.S. *America* for Paris.

A Débutant in Paris

Shivering on the deck of the S.S. *America,* my 130-pound frame presented a more rugged appearance than usual. Under my clothes was eight hundred dollars in fives and singles hidden in a money belt. Far below, in my tourist-class cabin, I'd stowed a Navy parachute bag packed with nylon stockings and soap ... rare as diamonds in Europe, I'd been told.

As the Manhattan skyline dissolved into the mist, black doubt descended. Could a person live in Paris for a year on eight hundred dollars plus seventy-five a month from the G.I Bill? Could this person with no French at all bluff his way through a year at the Sorbonne?

"No, you fool," muttered the Statue of Liberty through the gloom.

Ellis Island appeared. The place where my grandparents had entered America ... the place where Dovid Seltzer had become the more American and ritzier David Goldenberg.

Among my cabinmates, two were also veterans on their way to Paris to take advantage of the G.I. Bill. Both spoke some French.

Jake Turgeon was a struggling actor. Bob Brown was a struggling journalist.

When I told Bob I was heading for the Sorbonne, he said, "They don't speak English there. You'll be like a six-year-old Chinese at Harvard." With great patience, he tried to teach me some French.

I learned *pourquoi* and *parce que* and *des oeufs sur le plat,* but we were both aware that "why," "because," and "fried eggs" couldn't get you through college.

It was raining when we reached Le Havre. A difficult time. Bob's French was not too effective against real Frenchmen. We finally got through customs (he, too, had brought a hoard of stockings and soap to barter) and onto the boat train for Paris.

The City of Lights was cold, dark, and wet. We searched for a cheap hotel—sometimes carrying our heavy, cumbersome luggage and sometimes dragging it. In a small restaurant, we ate a meal listed as rabbit. Bob thought it was roast *chat.*

"The first thing we're going to do," he said, "is unload our booty. Get cash, travel light."

We finally checked into the Hotel St.-Père in St. Germain des Près.

The porter, a friendly chap, showed us to our room ... dark wood, brass beds, huge armoire. We were mystified by the bidet.

"*C'est pour madame!*" He laughed.

"This guy is okay," Bob said. "Maybe we can deal with him. Porters are very big in the black market."

I agreed. As Bob and the porter haggled over the transaction, I observed, proud to have a friend who could do business in French.

The deal was concluded. The Frenchman departed with soap and nylons, leaving us with reams of francs ... blue-and-green tissue-paper money. With pen and pad we began to calculate our profits. We had bought the treasure in New York, transported it across the Atlantic, and sold it in Paris at a loss.

The next few days were sunny. I wandered about, drunk with beauty ... parks, boulevards, cafés, and shops. A dream. All swimming in Paris sauce ... a cloud of flowers and river smell and garlic.

Slowly, we learned how to make phone calls, how to use buses and subways, how to get to American Express for mail and, later, to the American Embassy for checks.

We found that the hotels on Boulevard Montparnasse were cheaper than the St.-Père. At the Hotel États-Unis, we found rooms for eighty cents a day. To bathe, you sponged out of your bidet or went to the public bath in the Gare.

The États-Unis was the headquarters for Gary Davis and his "Citizen of the World" movement. Gary, the son of a fashionable East Coast orchestra leader, had rejected his U.S. citizenship in protest against war. He attracted many followers: French, American, German, and English.

High excitement! All day long, visitors ran up and down the narrow stairs of the États, committees were formed, and people interviewed ... each other. Then with great hue and cry, Gary himself would appear in his worn Air Force jacket.

Every evening in the little café on the street floor, an accordion played. Girls arrived. We couldn't get their attention. They weren't interested in fellows who were citizens of anywhere.

Bob decided to spend his days before the Sorbonne opened writing an article on Gary, hoping to sell it to the United Press. I was on my own. I ran into Jake Turgeon. "You guys are real tourists," he said. "You're still hanging around with other Americans. You'll never get the flavor of French life."

He told me he was living with a French family, speaking only French. Also, there was a very attractive daughter involved. Something big would develop there at any moment. He left me wearing invisible tourist cameras hanging from my neck.

On registration day, we strolled down Boulevard Montparnasse, through the Luxembourg Gardens and across Boulevard St. Michel to the Sorbonne. There, seven hundred years of shuffling students had worn paths in the clammy stone floors.

Our course was a special one for foreigners: the *Cours de Civilisation Français pour les Étrangers*. We'd be put in various subgroups, depending on our French capabilities. Bob registered for the middle group. As I tried to answer the clerk's questions, he turned to Bob. I had told him I was eighty-two years old. He put me in the lowest group.

For several days, I attended the bottom class. But even there, I had no idea of what was being said. When my name was called, I'd stand to reply, but never understood the question. It was not only embarrassing, but I feared I would lose my subsistence checks and have to go home.

Fortunately, I was not alone. There were other dumbbells. A special class was formed, called *Les Débutants*. We marched through dark old stones to a small classroom in the Galerie Victor Hugo. It may have once been a janitor's bin or a torture chamber ... plain wooden benches, small dungeon windows high on one wall.

Our professor was Mademoiselle Vidal, a tiny, ancient, hunchbacked lady in heavy black clothing; a wide black hat was fastened to her head by a huge pin. Rays of light coming through the dirty windows illuminated her white moustache.

She tapped her pointer on the board. Written there were the words *"le petit chaperon rouge."*

"I know what that means," one of the *débutants* whispered. "It's 'Little Red Ridinghood.'" We were a very basic group.

Mademoiselle never uttered a word of English. We often wondered if she could. Her patience was saintly. Her method was to teach us children's stories from a little book. One was assigned certain stories. Somehow you learned them. You were able to stand on command and recite them. Sometimes you even understood them.

My big numbers were *"Mon Bon Chien, Balto"* and *"Une Hardie Perroquet."*

After a while, people began to ask me to do my recitations outside of school. I did "My Good Dog, Balto" and "A Hardy Parrot" at the Dôme and at the Deux Magots restaurants and once at a dinner party. I did them as well as I could. People found them hilarious.

Life was pleasant. I was clinging to my niche at the Sorbonne, and almost living within my budget. My afternoons were free to roam Paris. I couldn't get enough of it.

What was it that held me spellbound? Ravel and Debussy and Renoir and Lautrec and Zelda and Isadora and Victor Hugo and George Gershwin had prepared me for something wonderful, and it was. I saw little of the meanness usually attributed to Parisians. People were generally kind, responding to my conversation with smiles. A Frenchwoman explained, "You are grown man but speaking like baby."

Even though I wasn't getting quite enough to eat, the food in our little student restaurants was delicious. But there were other unfulfilled needs.

Here I was in the most romantic city on earth and hadn't had one emotional experience. Bob had joined forces with a lovely Swedish girl from his class. I couldn't communicate with the French or German girls, couldn't find just the right Swede, and the Americans seemed loud, metallic, and excessively wealthy.

I bumped into Jake Turgeon, now so Frenchified he seemed hardly to remember English. I was made to understand that he was sleeping with the stunning daughter where he was living.

I told him I was hoping to meet a nice Swedish girl because they all spoke English.

"Tourist!" he snarled.

The days grew warmer, the air softer. And, as always during earthbound periods of my life, I became obsessed with flying. In my little room in Montparnasse, I dreamed of girls and flying.

One day, at the États-Unis, I met Guy Marchand. He had been an F.F.I. fighter pilot and was now working with Gary Davis. Guy held the French endurance record for *vol à voile* . . . the French term for soaring, riding air currents in powerless aircraft. The art had been invented by the Germans between the wars. I had grown up reading about this, desperately wanting to do it. Guy had captured a standing air wave over the Alps, flying solo for forty hours.

A small, fiery fellow with a red beard, he told me that students could be subsidized by the French government. One could fly gliders for a dollar an hour.

Shortly after my encounter with Guy, things seemed to look up in the romance department. One afternoon, I had decided to explore the Parc des Buttes-Chaumont. The parks were gradually undergoing restoration to their prewar glory. Once again, gardeners were engaged in topiary work. Bushes were shaped into castles, hemispheres, and animals.

I paid ten sous to the uniformed attendant, permitting me to rest on a bench. The green garden was splashed with colors ... striped umbrellas and sails of toy boats on artificial miniature lakes.

After a moment, I was joined by a youthful nanny pushing a perambulator ... surely the Rolls-Royce of perambulators. She smiled. She had ivory skin, dark hair and eyes, a full figure, and seemed to be speaking Spanish. Her French was worse than mine. But no matter.

Soon we were holding hands. Butterflies frolicked, the baby gurgled, and I kissed the nanny.

What had begun as a simple bench-sharing warmed to passion, then flamed to lust. Hesitating slightly, she permitted me to guide her behind a bush in the shape of a hippopotamus. There, on a soft bed of leaves, we tore at each other's clothing. Her under-*pantalons* came off smoothly. So did mine. Then, as Chaucer said, "That dibble from which men are made came to attention and doffed his cap."

Suddenly, she leaped to her feet. *"Juif!"* she yelled. Then she fled, shrieking, *"Juif! Juif!"*

Panic possessed me. A headline in the Paris *Herald Tribune* appeared before my eyes: "*Juif* attacks Spanish *au pair* girl in hippopotamus bush."

But no one seemed to notice as she disappeared, pushing the Rolls-Royce through the Bolivar Avenue gate.

A close call! I decided to forget about *l'amour* and concentrate on learning to soar. The next afternoon, I found the Air Ministry.

There, no English was spoken. Just lightning-fast Gallic military talk. An official had decided that I was trying to get into the Foreign Legion.

"May I be of help?" a British voice asked.

A tall, blond Englishwoman introduced herself as Madame Girard. She was married to a French air force pilot, and had just returned from Algeria. I explained my problem. In a moment, we were in the office of the director of *Service de l'Aviation Légère et Sportive*. She explained to him that I was a commercial and military pilot in America, a student at the Sorbonne, and anxious to try *vol à voile*. In a moment, I had paid two thousand francs for a *carnet de vol à voile individuel* . . . four dollars! Four dollars to soar like the birds!

Mme. Girard was a creature of musical speech, vivacity, and charm. Very attractive. She suggested an *apéritif*. We spent a pleasant half hour under a café awning . . . she nursing a cognac and I, a bottle of warm apricot juice.

A pity she was married. I said goodbye, thanked her once more, and went to the États-Unis to plan my bus routes to the Centre de Vol à Voile de Beynes the following afternoon.

The Centre was a neat little grass airport surrounded by soft green hills. There was an office shack, four hangars, one ancient open-cockpit round-engine towplane,

A Débutant *in Paris*

and many gliders. From a peeling wooden hangar marked *Réparations* issued the only sound . . . loud arguments. "The mechanics," Guy explained.

Suddenly, a lovely cream-colored glider hurtled across the field into the air. I had heard no engine and seen no towplane.

Then I realized it had been launched by a winch, a huge reel of cable located on a truck over the hill. One of the students waved a long pole topped by a red disk, the signal that could be seen from the winch.

"They'll be glad to have you here," Guy explained. "Monsieur Raymond must practice English in order to teach Swedish students this summer. He will be your *moniteur*."

In a moment, a dual trainer landed. Guy introduced me to Monsieur Raymond, a stocky fellow with a happy disposition and French dentistry . . . a large elf with a mouthful of lead bullets.

"*Formidable*," he said. "We speak only the Englitch." Then he was off to another glider, where another student awaited him.

When not flying, the students were busy returning the cable from the winch and moving gliders from place to place. I joined in. Thus began a happy time. Mornings at the Sorbonne. Afternoons at Beynes.

On my third afternoon, Monsieur Raymond took me up for my baptism. We donned parachutes, climbing side by side into a trainer.

The cable was hooked to the nose. Monsieur Raymond nodded to the *garçon* holding the signal pole. As he waved it, I could barely hear the winch motor. Then it rose in pitch. We were swept off the ground, climbing at an angle which would have been disastrous in a powered plane. I stiffened, expecting a stall.

"Nothing bad." Monsieur Raymond laughed, slapping my knee. "Everything marches okay."

Directly over the winch, the cable released with a pop. Then we floated over gentle green fields crisscrossed by white stone walls. Silent flight! Only the whisper of wind which rose to a murmur if you dove. More akin to the flying dreams of childhood than an airplane.

From two hundred meters, we were able to circle the airport three times before landing. In a heavy plane such as the Dauntless dive bomber, which I had sometimes flown in the Navy, two hundred meters would have meant a short glide to the ground.

Gently, Monsieur Raymond touched the plywood bird to earth. We rolled to the exact location from which we had started.

"Beautiful!" I said. "It's like . . ."

"Rita Hayworth," said Monsieur Raymond.

Later, as we waited for the Simca bus to take us back toward Paris, I noticed a marble plaque imbedded in the ground. The word "Heroes" stood out.

"Heroes?" I asked Guy.

"Rudder departed glider. *Mécanicien* forgot cotter pins. Hit here." He pointed to the plaque. *"Dommage!"*

"Heroes?"

"They avoided the office," he explained. I made a mental note to double-check the control hinges before each flight.

For the next ten afternoons, I went to Beynes; pushed gliders about, ate *jambon* sandwiches, and made short flights with Monsieur Raymond.

Controlling the glider was fun but tricky. Each landing had to be precise because there was no second chance. Such flying was close to nature. You smelled freshly mown hayfields, chicken farms, smoke from locomotives. To stay aloft, you prowled the sky seeking updrafts that burbled up from the sun-warmed earth.

I became good at it. I felt that without Monsieur Raymond's weight in the craft, I'd be able to fly a long time rather than three or four circuits around the field.

"I am ready now, Monsieur, to fly *tout seul.*"

"*Mais non.*" He shook his head. "It is not the custom. Not *avant quinze* sessions."

"But I do it well, *n'est-ce pas?*"

"*S'il vous plaît,* Everhart, I need to practice more the Englitch."

The next day, I followed the usual routine, repressing the urge to hound Raymond about going solo.

That night, Bob and his Kristin and I were dining at Chez Rosalie, a wonderful cheap little restaurant on rue de Vaugirard. He told me that his professor at the Sorbonne had asked him to pay Jake Turgeon a visit.

"They think he might be sick," Bob said. "He hasn't come to class in weeks. I have the address." We took the Seventy-two bus to Neuilly.

It was lovely there; modern apartment houses, hedges, and flowers. Shiny little automobiles parked on clean cobblestone streets. We found the house. The *concierge* put us on a little birdcage elevator. We rose to the fourth *étage.*

Jake himself answered the bell. For a moment, we failed to recognize him. He was thinner and wore a peculiar-looking haircut.

"Bob!" he said. "Everett! Come on in. Talk to me." We introduced Kristin.

"We can talk in here," he said, nervously herding us to a little sitting room. He shook our hands over and over again.

"The school is worried about you. Where have you been?"

"Well, you see . . ." He got up and closed the sliding doors. "I'm kind of involved here."

"Involved?"

Before he could answer, the doors slid open. A slender, hawk-faced girl poked her head through, glared briefly at us, and spoke to Jake.

"Jacob," she said, "don't dawdle. Wash for dinner. Helene and Charles are coming over for Monopoly later." Then the doors clicked shut and she disappeared.

"Is that . . .?"

Jake leaned weakly against the fireplace and nodded. "The daughter," he said. "I lied. She does speak a little English. I hate her guts."

"Why don't you leave?"

"It's like I told you. I'm involved. You know when I . . ." The doors flew open and Hawk-face was back.

"Jacob!" she said. "I thought I told you stay away from the *pâtisseries*." She held up a croissant. "This was in your room."

"I was hungry," he said, looking at the floor. The doors slammed together and she was gone.

"I just wouldn't stand for it," Bob said.

"You see"—Jake tilted a chair and revolved it on one leg—"I'm going to be a father."

After we left the fallen Francophile, we walked along the Seine as far as Trocadero, heartlessly laughing, skipping, and singing.

We were young, free, and in Paris.

The next day was crisp and clear. I was determined to fly solo.

"*Quel beau temps!*" I shouted to Raymond, pouncing off the bus.

At first I tried diplomacy. I told him I'd enjoyed every

moment of his company but didn't need any more lessons. I said his English had improved so much, one could mistake him for Anthony Eden.

"Solo . . . *tout seul!*" I begged.

Other students became interested in the discussion. Then they were joined by the mechanics, their high-pitched voices rising above the others. It was the same sort of collective group babble I had seen at French auto accidents.

"*Attention!*" Monsieur Raymond held up his arms.

A decision had been reached. He turned to me. "You may ascend alone," he said, "but it must be in an old machine, the *Peste du Ciel.*"

A stir in the crowd. "The *Peste du Ciel!*" they shouted, "the *Peste du Ciel!*" In a few minutes, chuckling and talking excitedly, they dragged it out. It was a red single-seater, covered with dust, having no canopy over the cockpit and no spoiler flaps on the wings. They pushed it into position for the hook, helped me into a parachute, and strapped me into place.

Then each one shook hands with me. Raymond gave me last-minute instructions. "She stalls on thirty-five kilometers. Fly always faster!" Then he, too, shook my hand. One of the hairy little girls they called "Minus" came over and kissed me. I was ready.

They put the hook on and raised the pole. The signal was lowered. I lifted into the sky like a ten-cent kite in a windstorm. It felt fine. I climbed strongly above the winch. It was time for the hook to snap loose.

I waited, suddenly noticing that my feet were shaking with excitement against the pedals.

And I waited. . . .

Suddenly, the *Peste* began to buck. It slammed up and down like a skiff against a heavy sea. The wings creaked.

I thought I was going to lose them. Just as the hook snapped loose, the stick jerked out of my hand.

For a second, the machine hung motionless, nose high. Then it stalled. I let it dive to pick up flying speed, recovered control, circled the field, and slide-slipped in for a landing. Raymond ran to greet me. I made a motion with my hand like a bucking bronco. "What happened?"

"Pardon, Everhart." He shook his head in self-accusation. "I forgot to say. It is a disease of the type. One must force down over the winch."

I made several flights in the *Peste* that day, taking her diseases into account. You had to lower her nose at the top of the tow. You had to glide her at a high speed to keep her from mushing down like a sick pelican. The Plague of the Sky ignored upcurrents. She just kept going down. Soaring was not her forte. She wanted to get back into that hangar to sleep. I wanted nothing more to do with her.

I refused to fly the *Peste* again. I wanted to climb into one of the cream-colored teardrops with the plastic hoods. A day like this blue-sky day was made for such a *planeur,* the Mouche.

There were two of them. One was at rest, warming its haunches in the sun. I ran my hands fondly over its seamless fuselage. Raymond was standing behind me.

"*Peut-être,*" he said.

"Hot dog!" I said.

"*Saucisson,*" he said. "I will speak with Directeur Le Pense." He went to the office.

Full of great expectations, I began to check over the Mouche, examining control surfaces, hinges, cotter pins, pulleys, and turnbuckles.

"*Très sage!*" Monsieur Le Pense commented. He was a spindly bureaucrat visiting that day from the Air Ministry. Raymond had brought him over to talk to me. My preflight inspection had made a good impression.

"*D'accord!*" he said.

Raymond, the *bon homme,* shared my joy. He gave instructions to have the craft pulled into launch position.

"*Un moment!*" he shouted, disappearing into the office. He returned with a small cedar box, winding a brass key on its side. I knew it was a recording barometer, but didn't understand my need for it. He placed it in a compartment behind the cockpit. In a moment, I was ready.

"*Maintenant!*"

The Mouche climbed effortlessly. Over the winch, the hook released on schedule.

Free of the cable, she had a flat, clean glide, flying smoothly. I saw some instruction flights spiraling upward and slid beneath them. They were in rising air. The Mouche was lighter and more efficient. At a thousand meters, I rose above them, waving and shouting. They returned the greeting.

For a moment, the thermal gave out and I began to lose altitude. Then, seeing several buzzards circling, I joined them. We climbed together.

Exhilarated, I lost track of time. For a moment, the thought crossed my mind that I was being selfish about the Mouche. As I rose above the buzzards, they watched me out of the corners of their eyes.

Now I was in the shadow of a quickly forming cumulus cloud. Strong lift . . . irresistible to the Mouche and to me.

Soon I was scraping the dark belly of the cloud. By squeezing back on the stick, I could disappear into it, then drop back at will. After half an hour of this cloud game, I realized that I was lost, cold, and goofy from lack of oxygen.

I located Paris on the horizon, turned to the compass heading from Paris to Beynes, and started down into heavier, more sensible air. When I found the field off to my left, shadows on the ground were long. Evening was approaching.

Shivering, I pulled the spoilers, circled down, and bounced to a landing.

As I climbed out of the cockpit, there were bravos and slaps on the back. Raymond removed the barometer from the fuselage, taking it into the office.

I was helping the others push the Mouche into its hangar when he returned with Directeur Le Pense.

"*Mes compliments!*" said Le Pense, pinning a small blue enameled medal to my shirt. I had won the "Silver C" of the International Soaring Society.

The next afternoon, low clouds hung over the city. There would be no flying. I wandered about the Bois de Boulogne. A soft, hazy day. Everywhere graceful girls sauntered about in colorful gossamer dresses and straw hats. Their musical voices filled me with wildness. I walked along the Seine.

There was Madame Girard, the tall English lady who had helped me at the Air Ministry. She wanted to know how I had progressed with my soaring. I told her all about it.

Suddenly, quite out of context, she said, "Don't you fancy me?"

"Oh, my God, yes, of course!"

"Then why didn't you ask me to sleep with you that day?"

"You're married!"

"Oh, that's done with. Finished!"

"But, me? There must be thousands of great-looking French guys who would love . . ."

"Filthy little frogs!" she blurted. We were under a bridge. "I'm off the little buggers. Never again!" She put her arms around me.

Under normal circumstances, I would have led her into a discussion of irrational prejudice and its possible international ramifications. But my brain, suddenly deprived of its blood supply, had gone apolitical.

Under the bridge, there was frenzied clutching. Irregular breathing. She had checked out of her hotel and was catching a boat train to London in an hour. The États-Unis was miles away.

My first Paris sexual event began from a standing start. Under the circumstances, it worked out nicely.

An old man and a dog watched, smiling. *"C'est très bon,"* one of them said.

Good Evening, Friends of Radio in the Greater Buffalo Area

With any sort of financial encouragement, I would have been happy to spend the rest of my life in Paris. Even though my original stake of eight hundred dollars was abetted by the G.I. Bill, a year of cautious living couldn't save it from fatal attrition.

Bob Brown found a job with United Press. He and Kristin were apartment dwellers, living in what we then called sin.

Everyone envied a kid named Art Buchwald. As restaurant and nightclub reporter for the Paris *Herald Tribune,* he not only received a small salary, but could take girls out to eat without paying.

Irving Block, the painter, was subsidized by a California patron—not too generously, it seemed. Attending the American ambassador's annual Fourth of July garden party, Irving rolled up his T-shirt, filled it with hors d'oeuvres, and ran off to his hotel room.

I might have called upon my father for funds. But I was resolute. Independence was his religion. I felt that asking for money would have made me hostage to the tire store. I was terribly thin, and, with a hundred thirty-five dollars remaining, it was time to go home.

All I could afford was cargo ship to Canada and coach train to Buffalo. The North Atlantic was cold, rough, and interminable. Eventually, I arrived in Quebec with a slight case of flu. With no direct train to Buffalo, I had to wait two hours in Utica, New York, for connections. I walked down Main Street.

I had forgotten the look of Downtown, U.S.A. ... neon signs, used-car lots, billboards, wires, poles, asphalt shingles, and peeling paint. My God, after Paris, Utica was ugly! Buffalo would be worse.

But family warmth mitigated culture shock. My Father, Sisters, Husbands, and Babies welcomed me. I slept late and ate, as they said on Buffalo's William Street, "like a dog." Soon I had put on ten pounds.

Now it was time to "write." My old friends, Maurice and Honora Simon, set aside a desk for my portable typewriter in their attic. Each day I went to my "office," figuring a reasonable output to be a story a week. I never knew how the stories would end when I started them, but I always worked something out. For several weeks, the story I finished on Saturday morning, I confidently mailed off to the *New Yorker*. If they were foolish enough to turn it down, I gave *Esquire* a chance at it. If *Esquire* missed their opportunity, I'd punish them by letting *Harper's* or *The Atlantic* have it.

As my collection of impersonal printed rejection slips grew, I began to realize that the stories were absolutely rotten.

Production slowed. Sometimes they took two weeks. Sometimes a month. Finally, one Saturday, I realized that I had spent a week in the office asleep with my head on the desk. I took my portable home and never returned.

Except for baby-sitting, I became a drone, wandering about the zoo and going to the library to listen to records, especially modern composers. My poor father knew I hated the store but tried to make his invitations sound literary. "You could come downtown to write up orders," he suggested.

One afternoon, I wrote to Bob Brown in Paris. The old portable was on the dining-room table. My little nephew Bruce sat on my lap. The baby loved watching typewriter keys flick words onto paper. The letter finished, I slipped a clean sheet into the machine. I wrote about my experiences learning to soar in France. I mailed it to *Air Trails*, the Street and Smith flying magazine.

It never came back. Nor did a rejection slip. A check for two hundred and eighty dollars came back. My father was bewildered. He looked at my typewriter on the dining-room table. He looked at me and at the check. "This is some nice business," he said. "You don't have any overhead."

When *Air Trails* came out, Gene Brooks, a friend in radio, suggested that he could arrange an interview on the "Bud and Mrs." talk show to promote circulation of the magazine. Bud was the surviving member of the radio comedy team "Stoopnagle and Bud," which had started in Buffalo during the thirties and gone national.

I understood that I was to arrive at WBEN, atop the

Statler Hotel, for an early morning rehearsal. There was friendliness, coffee, and cakes. Then we stood up to microphones for a jolly chat. I was nervous and slightly wild. The rehearsal ended. Through wall loudspeakers, the "Polka Parade" began.

"Thank you," Mrs. Bud said. "That was lovely."

"When do we do it?"

"That was it."

Turning hotly red, I apologized. But they said they were pleased. A bald young man with heavy horn-rimmed spectacles entered the studio. "I'm Ray Wander," he said. "I'm a producer here. Would you like to be the guest star on a TV play tomorrow night?" Too ignorant to be frightened, I said I would.

"The Clue" was Buffalo's weekly dramatic TV effort: fifteen minutes long, "live," and very low budget. Ray wrote the scripts. For the guest-starring role, I was to receive eight dollars. Jim Tranter, the lead, got fifteen.

The story followed the same format each week. A crime is committed. Everyone is baffled except Jim Tranter, playing Steve Malice, the detective. After the final commercial, he produces the Clue (usually a smoldering cigar), solving the case. Hearing my interview with Mr. and Mrs. Bud, Ray thought he might be able to do a comedy "Clue" he had written, featuring a character who collects stuffed birds.

Not knowing how to act, I ad-libbed my role. People said that, although I was terrible, they enjoyed watching a talented amateur get out of trouble.

Thereafter Ray also wrote commercials for me to do, in which I played various characters I developed. One I called "Dr. Sorgesson," a name I had stolen from Benchley. He spoke like the comedy actor, Charlie Butterworth. Another was Groucho and another was Mortimer Snerd. I got twelve dollars for each commercial.

In the fall, Ray was able to talk an independent station, WKBW, into letting me have my own radio show. There was to be no pay, but they would give us acetate recordings of each performance. They didn't like my name. For a while I was Everett Griswold. It didn't seem to work, so we tried Everett Echils (Aunt Leah's name). Wiseacres started calling me Everett Echilbaum. Eventually, we settled down to my real name. The show became known as "Greenbaum's Gallery."

With my two hundred and eighty dollars from the glider story, I bought a tweed Norfolk jacket. I already had two nice blue suits with ghosts of stripes on the arms from their days as naval uniforms. The rest of the money went for a 1937 Plymouth Sedan with no floorboards, no shock absorbers, and mushrooms growing out of the ceiling. You could watch the street go by as you looked down between your legs. The car rocked like a rowboat in a heavy sea. It made everybody nauseous except me and Ray Wander, who, too nervous to learn to drive, adored being "taken about."

Two things had kindled a glimmer of hope in my father's heart. First, he'd actually heard "Greenbaum's Gallery" on his car radio driving through Erie, Pennsylvania. "They got you going out of town," he said. And Nat Rumizen, who played gin rummy with him at the club, a man "in show business" (accountant for an advertising agency), told him I had a funny voice and the minute I learned to tell good jokes, I'd become wealthy.

The least he could do, as a parent, was to help me on my way.

With the understanding that a temporary measure had to be taken to relieve my fiscal needs—just until my "big break"—I worked down at the store two days a week. My hours in the tire game seemed even longer than they had during my disciplinary employment there as a child. To protect my image as a star, I managed to work most of the time in the basement.

My duties were to stack and unwrap tires, uncrate and assemble bicycles, and clean out repossessed refrigerators to expunge their smell. My mind did not attend. It busied itself conjuring up comedy notions for "Greenbaum's Gallery."

The show went on live each Sunday evening. We had two turntables for sound effects and music, a studio organ, a staff announcer, an engineer, and five or six different "characters," all, I'm afraid, obvious variations of my own Buffalo nasal vocal equipment.

From the beginning, we eschewed recordings from the hit parade, a practice which created our first enemies: the song pluggers. We played short works of Stravinsky, Milhaud, Poulenc, Ibert, and Delius. We played old musical-comedy numbers and Jolson and Chevalier. We played Sir William Walton's "Facade Suite," sometimes with Edith Sitwell's words, sometimes with mine.

From the chords of "Tea for Two," which Boozer had taught me on Majuro, I composed a lively ditty which became our theme. As I played it on the studio organ, the "steam calliope" stop pulled full out, the smooth-talking professional announcer, Cy Buckley, began, in his smooth-talking professional announcer's voice ... "Good evening, friends of radio in the greater Buffalo area, welcome once again to 'Greenbaum's Gallery': thirty minutes of good music and distinguished commentary on contemporary American living."

Of course, the distinguished commentary turned out to be madness; sometimes funny, sometimes dull, and sometimes in really bad taste. Today, when I watch young people doing the "Saturday Night Live" TV show, I share their triumphs and disasters.

Still, fearful of "acting," I ad-libbed the comedy segments from shirt cardboards upon which Ray and I had scrawled notes. We knew where certain favorite lines would be said, as well as cues for sound effects and music. We were influenced by Bob and Ray, Henry Morgan, Vic and Sade, Benchley, Thurber, and Perelman. Ray especially liked science fiction, old movies, and progressive jazz.

We did things like "Greenbaum's Gallery of Cowardly Dog Stories," "An Evening on Waikiki with Greenbaum's Hawaiians," and "Greenbaum's Gallery of Supernatural Stories." The latter, using Buffalo as a locale, usually began with giant crabs coming out of Lake Erie over the breakwall.

Several establishment Buffalo disc jockeys broadcast editorials against the "smart aleck" who was poking fun at the wonderful people to whom they owed so much: their friends of radio in the Buffalo area. Radio-time salesmen told Ray he was ruining his reputation. They refused to attempt to sell me to advertisers.

"Ev," Ray said to me after we had been on for three months, "the smell of death is everywhere."

The following Tuesday, the ratings, then called "Hoopers," came out. Incredibly, the audience was listening to me rather than to the competition. WGR, the ABC station, made an offer. Thirty-five dollars cash per show. First, Ray took me to a law firm, where I signed a paper giving him 40 percent of everything I would make. Then we crossed the street, took the elevator to the top of Buffalo's skyscraper, the Rand Building, and accepted.

Now we were in the Big Time. Ray was summoned to a meeting of the Brass, which excluded me. He emerged with the new rules. From then on we would use an "approved" script. And, instead of my "voices," we would have a cast of actors. We were permitted to keep Cy Buckley, but added a fine English actress from Toronto, Sheila Cox. In my role on "The Clue," I often had a prized stuffed bird snatched from my grasp by a giant Irish villain, played with great comic skill by an actor named Jim Murphy. He, too, joined us.

We were on Sunday evenings for a year. Every pay day, when I received my thirty-five-dollar check, Ray trotted me down to the bank on the first floor to receive his fourteen-dollar cut. He had an amusing way of putting it in his breast pocket, patting it, and saying, "My boutonniere money."

Very often, the show was good. The approved script, however, inhibited me in the writing and brought out my amateur status in acting. We were still getting acetate disks of each show. The use of tape hadn't reached Buffalo at that time.

After each successful show, I mailed the disk to the William Morris Agency. I began to receive encouraging letters from an agent named Harvey Orkin, in New York. He thought I belonged there.

Our Hooper rating slid slowly downward. Finally, the station needed our time slot for a religious program. "Greenbaum's Gallery" was canceled.

Fred Lounsberry, the owner's son, and Ray explained the situation in radio language. "The show simply doesn't seem to be going anywhere," Fred said.

"That's it, Everett," Ray echoed. "You're not going anywhere."

I pulled myself up straight in my Norfolk jacket. "Yes I am," I said without shame. "I'm going to New York to be a star, and you'll all be sorry." I strode toward the door. After all, there were larger worlds to conquer.

"Oh, Ev!" Ray called. I stopped. "Once in a while, if you'll come back to play the bird man, we'll give you twelve dollars and transportation."

"Okay," I said.

The Day I Killed Weintraub

The night before my departure, the whole family came for dinner. Sister Sylvia's husband, Everett Barlow, remarked: "You'll see. Ev's going to make it this time. He's going to be a success."

"May I live to see the day." Aunt Lil Greenbaum shoveled some of her sweet-and-sour cabbage onto my plate. "Take more. You'll need it."

For the second time since the war, I rode the Empire State Limited into Manhattan to do battle. For this attack, I thought myself well armed: seven hundred dollars' worth of traveler's checks, thirty pounds of acetate disks of "Greenbaum's Gallery," and a packet of fan letters . . . several of them written in ink.

For seven dollars a week, I rented a room on Fourteenth Street which might have served as a stage setting for Maxim Gorky's *Lower Depths*. But everything a fellow needed was nearby: the Automat, a Chinese laundry. Right down the hall were a pay phone and a bathroom. There was even a strong older woman to be wary of: my landlady, Mrs. Zweigert.

She was a small, stout, bustling little person of great tightness ... tight of clothing, tight of purse, and skin so taut it glistened. Her eyes bulged as though forced outward under pressure. A pituitary alarm told her when a tenant had made the forbidden substitution ... seventy-five-watt bulb for twenty-five. Without knocking, she would plunge into the room to unscrew the larger bulb, blurting, "Edison is rich enough already."

If she felt I was sleeping too late, Mrs. Zweigert would wake me up. One morning, she burst through the door, trembling with rage. "She done it! She done it, the dirty tramp!"

"What?"

"She run off with that goddamn Wop!" Ingrid Bergman had taken up with Roberto Rossellini.

To insiders, Harvey Orkin, the William Morris agent who had suggested I come to New York, was already a famous wit. He would soon be an international agent, representing Elizabeth Taylor, Richard Burton, and Peter Sellers. In England, he'd become a talk-show celebrity, known as the "American Master of the Byronic Aside." Like so many of the people in my life, he was to die young, after which Bernard Slade would base a successful play called *Tribute* on his life.

This was unknown to me as I approached his office in midtown. A scintilla of doubt sparked in my head. Had his encouraging letters been but a polite way of answering hopefuls who had mailed audition records to the agency?

Not to worry. He greeted me happily.

Nimble, black curly hair and glasses, quick-talking, with a voice like a burlesque straight man, Harvey was dynamic. It was wonderful to have someone with friends in high places planning my career. "Now, the first thing you're going to do . . ." he rubbed his capable hands together, "is to apply for unemployment insurance." Eager to please, I headed downtown.

The next day I returned to his office, a beaten man.

"What happened?"

"Harvey, they turned me down for Unemployment. The humiliation . . . the filth . . . the poverty. Coming down the stairs I saw this depressing sign offering to buy your blood."

"What were they paying?"

"Twenty-two dollars a pint."

He grabbed the phone in his strong agent's hands. "I'll get you twenty-six fifty!"

"I don't know. Maybe I'm better off in Buffalo."

"Hold everything. Trouble is, you're lonely. Know any girls?"

"No."

"You're having dinner with Miss America."

"Are you crazy?"

"Here's the address." He scribbled. "It's Adolph Green's apartment. Miss America will make dinner for you."

"Harvey, I . . ."

"Bye. Call me tomorrow."

The apartment was on a fashionable street that had somehow pluckily sprouted trees. In an entryway of marble and brass, I located a magic name: Adolph Green. Comden and Green had written several smash musicals. So far, Harvey's incredible plan for my evening had materialized. I pressed the button. "Come on up."

A sweet voice. But a Miss America voice?

I left the elevator and knocked on the door. It was opened by a girl. Pert, astonishingly pretty, wearing tight jeans, Jo-Carroll Dennison, Miss America 1942, rendered me speechless. Calling on old reflexes, I attempted a joke.

"Please don't tell me any jokes," she said. "I just divorced Phil Silvers."

Green's apartment was wonderful. Books and records everywhere, comfortable furniture, intriguing art. During dinner, Jo-Carroll told me about her life. I was fascinated.

The doorbell rang. Without interruption, Jo pressed the buzzer, shortly admitting a small gentleman in his early fifties, wearing granny glasses, tweedy clothes, and a moustache. She waved a hand toward him carelessly. "Everett Greenbaum, Sid Perelman."

My God, S. J. Perelman, wizard of the funny essay, ringmaster of the English language. At the crack of his whip, words danced with wit. I'd once spent three years looking for one of his books, *Dawn Ginsberg's Revenge.* This was like finding myself standing in the same room with Charles Dickens.

He spoke in perfect sentences, and knew everything. I don't know how we got on the subject, but he discoursed on a breed of dog indigenous to the Côte d'Azur, dogs noted for their large testicles. After a while, I sensed that Jo-Carroll was being neglected and that S. J. probably preferred her exclusive attention. I made a polite departure. I never knew if Harvey thought of that evening as a practical joke, but for me, it ended all thoughts of returning to Buffalo.

From time to time, Harvey welcomed me into his beau monde. One party he took me to was in the penthouse of Matty Fox, atop the Universal building. Fox was president of Universal at the time. There were almost as many butlers as guests. The silver and glass were all etched with Matty's cachet: a young fox in repose. After the party, still glowing with bits of clever talk, shards of piano music, and perfume of beautiful women, I returned to my seven-dollar-a-week room on Fourteenth Street. The contrast was dramatic.

One day Mrs. Zweigert appeared. I expected a bulb inspection, but it was a phone call from Warren Jacober of NBC, whom I had known in Buffalo. Once I'd taken him up in a rented plane and now he wanted me to fly camera crews to football games on Saturday mornings, returning with the exposed film in time to make the NBC evening news broadcast. I was delighted, and arranged to rent a Piper Tripacer.

Each Saturday morning, overloaded with camera equipment and personnel, we staggered into the brown air over Teterboro heading toward Cornell or Rutgers. Radio navigation was crude then and I always had to look around a bit for the right town. But I always found it and returned with game shots from the air and ground. The cameramen, highly strung fellows with wives and children, took the train home.

Warren arranged for a daredevil motorcyclist to meet me on the runway (enraging the tower), seize the film, and race with it to Rockefeller Center.

And I got fifty bucks.

Julian Claman worked for Talent Associates, the TV

producers. He and his boss, Al Levy, had listened to the records of "Greenbaum's Gallery" and decided to extend my life by giving me a small acting parts.

I never turned anything down. Once I was a body carried over a rooftop by the giant English actor, Francis Sullivan. On another show, I climbed the rickety rigging of a plywood sailing vessel. Once a white frightened face was required behind a window hit by a bullet. The shot effect was achieved by a spring device which shattered the window. I did the frightened face to perfection. The acting bits paid well for the time involved. And if you wore your own clothes you got a twenty-dollar wardrobe bonus.

Things were going so well that I rented a cold-water flat on Thompson Street in the Village. I was able to take young ladies to the films at the Museum of Modern Art and to feed them warm food from Gristede's. But it wasn't to last.

Without warning, the football season ended. Then acting parts dwindled, along with my income. I tucked the large disks of "Greenbaum's Gallery" under my arm and went out to beat the weeds of local radio.

One executive reacted favorably: Nat Rudick of WLIB.

"We don't pay a lot of money," he said. "Would you like to be on the 'American Israeli Festival'?"

I was reluctant to admit that although my ancestry is jam packed with Jews, I couldn't speak Yiddish or Hebrew. Finally I confessed.

"I know," he said. "You're a *yiddisha shagitz*. And that's the way we're going to bill you on the show."

And they did. The Yemenite announcer would say, "And here he is, the Yiddisha Shagitz from Buffalo"— meaning a person from Buffalo who was either a Jewish

Gentile or a Gentile Jew. The other performers were big names in Israel ... Shoshanna Damari and the drum-and-flute team, Hillel and Aviva.

Hillel was a dangerous-looking one-legged sabra. He constantly carved flutes out of bits of wood, wielding a wicked-looking knife.

I'd arrive at WLIB an hour before air time on Sunday afternoons, usually with a girl I was trying to impress. I would write three sketches, placing before each line the language in which it was to be spoken. The show consisted of an hour of comedy and music followed by an hour of serious drama. One Columbus Day the theme of the drama was that Columbus was really Jewish. I played Amerigo Vespucci, and was so overwhelmed by the incongruity of the thing that I giggled helplessly.

Sweet Aviva and the terrifying Hillel were hired to perform at the Blue Angel nightclub down in the Village. "Crazy guy there." Hillel broke into sudden hilarity. I didn't understand at first but gradually realized that there was a young fellow playing on the bill with them who was the funniest man Hillel had ever seen.

One night I went to the Blue Angel. The funny man was Wally Cox. I was bowled over by his offbeat, low-pressure, exquisite humor, and was astonished that Hillel was so attuned to him.

The "American Israeli Festival" never attracted a very large audience. In fact, I never met anyone who ever heard it outside of the engineer in the booth. Before the year ended, the show was dropped.

There were no acting jobs and no flying jobs, I still couldn't get unemployment insurance, and the rent was due. I had to mine thirty-two dollars and fifty cents out of the island of Manhattan to survive.

I heard that each December concessionaires hired

out-of-work actors to sell toys at the big department stores. Applying at Macy's, I soon found myself selling an item called Freddie the Jumping Frog.

It was a long-hours, strictly commission proposition. The concessionaire I worked for, Weintraub, stirred instant hatred. He was a blunt, five-o'clock-shadow, suspicious ferret of a man who seemed to feel that a soft word or a smile was a sign of weakness.

"Hea's whatcha gotta say." He squeezed a rubber bulb connected by a slender tube to a toy frog. "Ya gotta say," he continued in a flat, dull tone, "Getcha Freddie. Hea's Freddie the jumpin' frog. Fun. Fun. Fun. A barrelalaffs. Getcha Freddie the jumpin' frog!"

Then he left me with a parting remark. "Don't try to cop nothin'!"

Here at Macy's, there was no hiding in the basement, as at my father's store in Buffalo. Here you had to stay on your feet for ten hours shouting about Freddie Frog, dreading the routine visits of Weintraub, when he would hiss, "Getcha dollar volume up!"

Exhausted and bored, I squeezed two bulbs forcing two Freddies to swim happily around a large punchbowl of water.

"Here he is! Freddie the Frog. Hah hah. Fun fun." I croaked the weary litany.

But I was no better a salesman of frogs than of tires. At the end of three days, my hands were waterlogged, shriveled squids. The dreaded Weintraub no longer spoke to me but merely glared in passing.

About this time, word of my amphibious activities at Macy's filtered uptown to Warren Jacober at NBC. It triggered his natural impulse to do something big, impulsive, and funny. Something which people would talk about for years as part of his legend. He sent a man over to slip a dozen real frogs into my bowl while I was on lunch break.

When I returned from the sandwich machine, my fellow employees were showing a new, hilarious interest in my frog bowl. And no wonder. Some of my Freddies seemed to be jumping over into Ethnic Dolls, some into Educational Games.

A crowd gathered.

Weintraub appeared, the redness of blood pressure registering under his purple stubble.

"Gettout, ya bastid!" He pointed toward the down escalator. "Yer thru!"

My commission money! Two days before I had finally hit thirty-two fifty to pay the rent. I had sold a few more and now he owed me forty-three.

"My money," I said, holding out my hand.

"Fergit it! Ya done a hunnert bucks worth damage."

"My money. Pay me my money." The crowd watched this real-life drama. So did Weintraub's temporary help and the genuine full-time Macy's employees. Public opinion was on my side.

"Awwrite. Awwrite." Weintraub fished a dirty checkbook out of his pocket and scribbled the check with a pencil stub.

"Are you sure this check is good?" I asked.

"Bastid!" Weintraub turned his back on me and stomped away. Clearly I had hurt his feelings.

I deposited the check and sent one of my own to the landlord . . . just a week late.

Two mornings later I awoke, put on slacks, sneakers, sweatshirt, and blue Navy raincoat, went down the cold stone steps to the unheated lobby, and unlocked my mailbox.

Suddenly there was heat. Starting in my sneakers and

rising like red lava up my skinny legs to set my brain afire.

"No such account." The check was a fake. I ran out into the snowstorm, across Washington Square to the subway station on Sixth Avenue. Ignoring the snow falling on my head, I hurried because I was on my way uptown to kill Weintraub.

Connections were excellent. Without waiting I stepped directly from the uric haze of the station onto the express. One short stop at Fourteenth and then I was at Thirty-fourth Street, going up the escalator to the toy department.

Rage holding up nicely. No time for second thoughts. Everything working for me. Toy floor. Weintraub walking right toward me. I leapt at him, clutching my hands around his rotten little throat. Fury unleashed!

"Bad check!" I yelled. "Crook!"

He was reaching into his pockets. Probably for a knife, maybe a gun. I didn't care. Suddenly he began throwing money at me. A green flurry of bills settled to the floor.

I relinquished his throat and began gathering up cash. No one stopped me as I disappeared down the escalator clutching three twenties.

Once outside, head soaking and fevered, I walked through the snow aimlessly. After a while I found myself outside the Finnish restaurant on East Fiftieth Street. Talent Associates was upstairs. I went in.

"Thank heaven. We've been looking for you all day," the receptionist said.

"We've got a job for you," Julian Claman said.

"My clothes or theirs?"

"Doesn't matter what you wear," Al Levy said. "We're going to try you on a writing job for two weeks. Get in that office and write with Jim."

The show was "Mr. Peepers," starring Wally Cox. Jim was Jim Fritzell, the red-headed Viking, the button in the cap of kindness. He began to teach me the basics of situation comedy. There was magical rapport.

The two weeks on "Mr. Peepers" became three years. Then, except for my first two years in Hollywood, we would write together until his death, twenty-seven years later.

Wally

Wally Cox has been best described by his old gradeschool pal, Marlon Brando.

"Wally," he says, "was an embroidered Japanese robe with Three-in-One Oil stains on it."

I was unprepared for Wally. He was shy, almost terrified to find himself a celebrity. Several times I tried to engage him in conversation, but he vanished like a small, wild deer. Then something happened.

"Mr. Peepers" originated each Sunday evening before several thousand people in a wonderful place, the Center Theater at Rockefeller Center. This was before the invention of tape. What the TV audience saw was happening at that moment.

One hot spring Sunday, after the dress rehearsal, Wally remarked on the sad fact that the fine day had to be spent in a dark theater. I suggested that we take the observation elevator to the top story of Radio City in order to inhale a higher and possibly cleaner layer of New York air. We did this.

Wally, dreading the general public, insisted that we stay in a remote corner of the observation platform. Here, we made small talk until ten minutes before air time. It was then we discovered that the visitors had gone, the doors were locked, and we were stranded seventy stories above the stage. Around the United States, millions of people were turning on their television sets to see their beloved "Mr. Peepers," never dreaming that he was unavailable. In the control rooms of NBC ... panic. Technicians were threading up a standby film, "Reforestation in Minnesota."

Although Wally's TV image was a frail little fellow, under the wrinkles of that brown suit crouched a muscled hiker who was also brave.

"If we jump across that space," he said, "there is every possibility we can get through an open door to an elevator."

He indicated a two- or three-foot gap between sections of the roof. If you missed, you fell seventy stories. While I was still gasping, Wally leaped over.

Before allowing myself to think, I joined him. In a moment, we emerged from an express elevator into an unfamiliar lobby area of Radio City.

We were seized by guards. Not one of them had ever seen "Mr. Peepers." They thought we were thieves or saboteurs. Finally Wally persuaded them to consider our situation. One of them went with us to the Center

Theater. Two ushers and a script girl, part of a searching party, hailed us from across the street. Wally was escorted onto the stage, and the show was on. From that moment, we were friends.

If you knew Wally, you would come to know Marlon Brando.

Sam Gilman, an actor and acting teacher, had a large bachelor apartment off Sixth Avenue. On Friday evenings, he gave parties where Wally and Marlon were the guests of honor. Wally often took me along, both of us hoping we would meet attractive, passionate, and foolhardy girls.

At that time, Marlon was at the apex of his *Streetcar Named Desire* Broadway stardom. Wally and I went almost unnoticed as he waded among the ladies. It wasn't easy to relate to Marlon during that period. He was driven by strange self-destructive forces. One night, he asked a stagehand to box with him between scenes of *Streetcar*. The stagehand broke his nose. Marlon finished out the performance spurting blood, and spent a week in the hospital.

On Saturday afternoons, Wally and I drove up to Rockland County Airport, where I gave him flying lessons. He was an excellent student, soloed quickly, and then decided never to fly again. "I don't enjoy freedom in so many different directions," he said.

A complete original, Wally was an unregistered philosopher with his own modus vivendi. He never saw the need to own more than one suit, a dun-colored, Airedale-looking outfit. He carried a necktie in his pocket for entering restaurants and for "state occasions."

Practicality was the theme. He carried, besides bills, a certain combination of coins which would expedite all transactions with a minimum of fuss: a dime, a nickel, three pennies, and a quarter. I can't explain it to you, because I never understood it. He solved the problems of keys by soldering all of his keys into a star, the handles in the center, the shafts extending outward: a sharp, wicked thing to have in your pocket, but in its utility, very pleasing to him.

When "Mr. Peepers" ended, I moved to California and didn't see much of Wally for two years. Finally, he too moved west.

Outside his California house, phone bells rang in the trees. In the living room, he suspended a long rope so that he could swing across the room without touching the floor. "Some of my best lessons have been learned from cats," he said.

To walk with Wally was an education. He knew all the buds, all the birds and beetles, and could tell you amusing facts about them.

Once, while walking across a lawn with Marlon's sister, Jocelyn, Wally suddenly held up a cautionary hand for silence.

"What's the matter?" Jocelyn asked.

"An ant lion is poised to attack," he said. He had seen an insect known as the ant lion. He knew them all.

He knew birds, too. Before he had lived in an area for very long, he was able to call birds to eat out of his hand. At one California house, they even came indoors.

The first time Jocelyn met him, they were living in Evanston, Illinois. One day she came across a small boy who was tied to a tree and seemed resigned to his fate. Marlon had lashed Wally to a fir and gone off someplace. She untied him and became a lifelong friend.

Jocelyn treasures her memories of him. One day, as adults, they explored a field of wildflowers. Someone had warned them that there was a bear in the neighborhood. As they strolled through the field, Wally invented two "haiku" poems.

> Bear
> Stay there
> Beware
> I've a twig
>
> In the lair
> What is the hair?
> It is a bear
> Oh Lordy!

He created another one during an awkward moment at the beach.

> Young woman in bathing suit
> Why do you stand on the dock thus?
> Don't you want me to see the lake?

In the sixties, almost everyone in TV moved to California. I had married a soft-spoken southern girl who found Wally delightful. We didn't mind that he loved to come visiting without warning. On occasion, we would arrive home to find a bunch of twigs and leaves attached to the front doorknob. This meant Wally had stopped by and would return later.

Sam Gilman, on the other hand, still a bachelor, found the surprise visits inconvenient. "Wally," he begged, "please ... the next time you come, just pick up the phone and let me know."

A few days later, Sam heard the scuffle of feet on his porch. It was Wally. Sam stared at him.

"This is a phone call," Wally said.

His chance remarks were short and on target. Once I rented a sailboat. Sailing was one of his many skills, but he was nervous about being recognized by a gang of rough-looking fellows at the end of the dock. To board the boat, we would have to walk through them. He held back. "What's the matter?" I asked.

"There's a strong element of scoff out there," he said.

Another time, I arrived at his house to find twenty painters at work. Much labor is done in California by illegal aliens from Mexico.

"My God, Wal, how can you afford so many painters?" I asked.

"They work cheap because they are able to speak Spanish," he explained.

Wally's abilities beyond the comedic were amazingly assorted. He could whistle in two-part harmony. He could yodel beautifully, compose songs, and swim underwater longer than anyone.

He made jewelry of silver and gold. He built sturdy furniture, inlaying wood with brass. He studied languages and was familiar with French, German, Swedish, and Hebrew. He wired and plumbed his house in Rockland, New York. He read and understood every page of the *Scientific American*.

Wally and Marlon were boys together in Evanston. Later, in their New York struggling days, they shared a cold-water flat with a raccoon and several sets of electric trains. They had a rare and wonderful rapport, talking endlessly, seeking truth: truth about life and women and work, formulating theories to go by. In Wally's words, "We were great dopesters."

It was in California that I was sometimes included in these grand conversations. They were funny and shocking and very original. Both men could imitate anyone ... public figures, friends, animals, and even machines. Sometimes there was, as Mel Brooks calls it, *dangerous laughter*. You couldn't breathe, teetering on the edge of strangulation.

On the subject of marriage, one received the impression that each had worked out a formula for contentment. In practice, however, disaster was everywhere. Marlon's unfortunate alliances are legendary. Wally had two failed marriages before he met his Patricia.

Patricia Tiernan Livingston was the most unlikely woman one would expect to marry Wally Cox. Once a starlet of breathtaking beauty, she had been involved with some of the most glamorous men of her generation ... actors, politicians, financiers. She charmed them all: Harry Cohen, Henry Miller, Richard Burton.

Her story was one which seems to echo in Hollywood like a repeating loop of film. The girls change, but the plot remains the same. A lovely waif is brought up in foster homes, is raped at an early age by a foster father, wins a beauty contest, gets a movie contract, is eluded by fame, then the road down ... drink, dope, trouble. Pat had made several suicide attempts by the time she met Wally. The two found in each other sympathy and stormy happiness.

As Marlon put it, "This marriage is like a broken-down old car, but you can depend on it to keep going."

> Great wits are sure to madness near allied
> And thin partitions do their bounds divide.
> **DRYDEN**

To protect itself from the pain of a grain of sand, the oyster coats it with layers of nacre to make a pearl. In the same way, a psyche, to avoid pain, covers a neurosis with protective layers to make talent.
MARLON BRANDO

In the time of "Mr. Peepers," Wally had depressed days when he wasn't at his best. As he got older, these came more and more often. Vainly, he went from analyst to analyst. His great fear was that his friends would think they were in some way responsible for the black clouds.

In 1972, Wally and I wrote a children's book together. One day, in a fit of gloom, he stared into the grass outside the window in the alcove where we worked. He described to me all of the misery he saw there ... the greed, the cannibalism, the cruelty of nature, right there in the world of insects and growing things, where formerly he'd found joy.

He began drinking heavily. When he began to miss professional appointments, Pat knew it was time for action. She found a doctor who cured alcoholism by substituting tranquilizers for drink.

The results were dramatic. Wally was no longer depressed. He became dependable in his TV and movie work. Soon, our book was finished and sold to a publisher. We started on another book. Then, very subtly at first, but inexorably and cruelly, depression stalked him again. Alcohol was forbidden to anyone on the tranquilizer treatment, and he was cut off from that balm.

One day we were working at the heavy oak table Wally had made. The sun was pouring in. All the cats and dogs and the goat were behaving nicely. Amid the verdant lushness of the garden, the lissome Pat had come out of the pool and was sunning herself, wearing a towel.

Suddenly, Wally cleared his throat. "Say, old SuperEv," he said, "I think this is a good time to thank you for sticking by all these years ... for being my friend."

A wave of grief hit me. He seemed to be saying goodbye. Tears rolled down my cheeks.

"Oh, dear," he said, "I knew it. I've exceeded your sentiment threshold. Apple juice! Apple juice for all hands!"

He ran to get me a drink.

The depressions became darker and deeper. Sometimes Wally walked around the house all night while Pat slept. She was afraid he was drinking.

One morning she found him dead. The coroner's official verdict was heart attack.

Wally had wanted his ashes scattered to the four winds. Marlon took them into the dense woods, in the hills behind the house. He carried out his task. But later, he said he had saved some of the ashes to keep in a small container. "Just to talk to once in a while."

Chipping Away

"Mr. Peepers" delineated the life of a small-town high-school science teacher. In 1952, it was fashioned around Wally Cox by NBC producer Fred Coe, a man responsible for the early beginnings of a whole generation of America's actors, writers, and directors. Under his aegis, the format was created by David Swift, a former Disney cartoonist, and Jim Fritzell, a struggling California writer who'd collaborated with him on some TV scripts.

Ford Motors sponsored the show for eight weeks as a summer replacement. Quite unexpectedly, in the autumn, NBC received thousands of letters asking for its return. Reynolds Aluminum agreed to put it on Sunday evenings. Swift and Fritzell were retrieved from California.

From the beginning, there was conflict between Fred and David. The latter relished broad physical humor, i.e., toupees falling off, floor polishers running up walls, and so forth. Coe, even though a graduate of the Yale Drama School, was semiliterate. But he was an excellent producer, with a great love for talent and the theater. Mississippi-born, he was able to communicate the most subtle nuances of feeling in homespun terms. Despite his irascible nature, artists loved working with him. One felt in him the swamp ferment which had produced Tennessee Williams, Truman Capote, and Carson McCullers. His "Philco Playhouse" was the most successful dramatic anthology show on television. For "Mr. Peepers," he strived toward reality and humor springing from character. Jim Fritzell's instincts concurred, but he was unwilling to oppose David, his mentor.

As the three men departed the theater one day, a nerve-fraying argument raged between David and Fred. David threatened to leave New York, leaving the writing problems to Jim. Jim fell down on the sidewalk with a heart palpitation. David was not making an empty threat. He'd just married the young actress, Maggie MacNamara, then finishing her stage role in *The Moon Is Blue*. They went off to Italy, ending his active participation in the show.

For several weeks, an unsuccessful plan was tried wherein rough drafts by other writers were rewritten by Jim. In three weeks, he too decided to bolt, following an argument with Hal Keith, the show's director. In the East Side offices of Talent Associates, it was a time of crisis. David Susskind, Al Levy, and Julian Claman begged Jim to stay.

Julian remembered the pile of "Greenbaum's Gallery" records in the closet. "We'll get someone who can help you," he said. They began looking for me. And that was the day I appeared, soaked and half mad, out of the teeth of a snowstorm.

The odds against two people meeting who are able to write comedy successfully together are even worse than the odds against finding a perfect marriage partner. It is an absolute miracle! Many times, in the next quarter century, when things were going well for the team of Fritzell and Greenbaum, Jim would look at me, shake his head, and say, "We found you under a rock."

He was a first-generation American of Scandinavian parentage, raised in San Francisco. I'm a third-generation Jewish mongrel, raised in Buffalo. Yet we'd been marinated in the same American juices, had shared the same Judeo-Christian ethics and the same storehouse of clichés.

In San Francisco, when a fire engine raced by, sirens wailing, people said, "Probably they're going out to lunch." That's what they said in Buffalo! In Buffalo, when visitors from another town felt unwell, people said, "It's the change in the water." That's what they said in San Francisco.

Ninety percent of the time we agreed on what was funny. In complete rapport, we were like a team of acrobats communicating telepathically. One began a sentence; the other finished it.

In the beginning, Jim gave me writing lessons. I had been properly creating jokes and sketches on instinct, but now I had to learn to construct a story with conflict, a beginning, middle, and end, avoiding incredibility, coincidence, and *deus ex machina*. I discovered that professional comedy writers used trade expressions among themselves. A few examples of this argot are:

Kicked: Trite or overdone.
Reprise: To repeat words or actions for comic effect.
Treacle cutter: A joke at the end of an oversentimental moment to relieve tension.
Pissing in the milk: Adding unnecessary lines or action to a scene, diluting it.
Teaser: A short cliffhanger scene at the beginning of a show, intended to hold the audience through the first commercial.
Tag: A short, happy scene at the end of a show, intended to hold the audience through the last commercial.
Jack story: Umbrage taken by a character before justification exists.

After my trial period at fifty dollars a week, Fred Coe decided that we would dispense with the first drafts written by other writers. Then I got two hundred a week and screen credit, reading "Script: Jim Fritzell–Everett Greenbaum." Jim explained that I should be pleased because in Swedish "Jim Fritzell" meant "written by." In time to come, we would divide the money equally and alternate top billing.

For three years, we wrote forty shows a year—except for three or four missed because of illness. Our seven-day week began Monday morning with a meeting in Fred's Rockefeller Plaza office to decide on a story. Sometimes we arrived with a pocketful of notions, and it was easy. On other dark Mondays, it seemed impossible to dredge up anything ever again. But Fred was always encouraging, a great catalyst. He would begin to chat about the other characters on the show, played by such excellent actors as Marion Lorne, Pat Benoit, Tony Randall, Ruth McDevitt, Georgann Johnson, Jack Warden, and Reta Shaw. Soon, we'd hit upon a problem for one of them, and relate it to Mr. Peepers. Then, back to our office.

We wrote all day, hoping to finish ten pages by late afternoon. Jim called it "chipping away." Lunch was sent from the drugstore, to be wolfed down as we labored.

We were always involved in two scripts simultaneously, the "new"one and the rewrite of the next to be performed. Since the Xerox machine hadn't been invented, a company called Netzers mimeographed script copies. After we finished each script, Jim, exhausted and trembling, left it to me to have duplicates made. Late one evening, I emerged from the office glassy-eyed, clutching a script which we'd written in ten straight hours and jumped into a cab. "Netzers and step on it," I yelled to the puzzled driver.

Sunday was a big day. I would meet Jim at the empty office, where we finished the first draft of the "next" script by 3 P.M. Then he went home to watch the show, as I walked over to the Center Theater to deliver the script and see our dress rehearsal. Fred was shuttling between "Mr. Peepers" and "The Philco Playhouse," which also broadcast on Sunday evening. At dinnertime, we often went to Hurley's Bar, an old establishment which had refused to sell out to the Rockefellers. They'd had to build around it, with the result that Hurley's looked like a nasty bruise on a corner of Radio City.

Eating dinner, we could see lines of people waiting to watch the "Peepers" broadcast. When I returned to the theater, Bernie Green's orchestra was rehearsing the musical cues. The audience filed in—thousands of people. The show began. When the laughs began to tumble out of the balconies, rolling down the orchestra section to bristle the hairs on the back of my neck, I knew we had put the right words down on paper.

As we poured out material, it became necessary to dig deeper into oneself for nourishment. I found a source, oddly enough, in memories of French movies. They were full of wonderful bourgeois attitudes which had stayed with me. For example, in Jean Renoir's film *Boudu Saved from Drowning,* the husband complains, "I don't play the piano. You don't play the piano and the children don't play the piano. Why do we have a piano?"

The wife replies, "Because we're respectable people, that's why."

On "Mr. Peepers," this appeared in the form of Aunt Lil's boyfriend admiring her piano. "Do you like it?" she asks.

"It's not only educational, but it's dressy," he says.

The French realized that part of the generation gap is an education gap. In Marcel Pagnol's *Fanny,* Raimu, the bartender, is teaching the trade to his son. "You put in a third of gin, a third of vermouth, a third of lemon juice, and a great big third of water."

"There are only three thirds, Poppa. You can't put in another big third of water."

"Don't tell me," the father says. "I was a bartender before you were born."

In "Mr. Peepers," Aunt Lil sees her nephew as a graduate teacher for the first time. "Say something in General Science for me, Sonny," she begs.

"Aw, now, Aunt Lil," he says, shyly.

"Come on, after all, I changed your diapers. Now you can do something for me. Say something scientific. Please."

"Well . . . all right . . . capillary action!"

She gazes at him, enchanted.

"Mr. Peepers" was a hit. In the first season, the show won a Peabody Award, and we received an Emmy Award nomination for writing. Few joys are as delicious as sudden success following threadbare years. Spending money was exquisite. I bought clothes from Brooks Brothers, and moved from the cold-water flat on Thompson Street to a basement apartment just off lower Fifth Avenue. I bought a used MG so that, on rare days when work was finished early, I could drive to Staten Island to rent airplanes. Pursuit of girls combined nicely with theater and dining out. Each week, I got a letter from my father telling me to save enough to pay an obligation which had never been my concern . . . the income tax.

On our first week of the summer layoff, I returned to Buffalo. Ray Wander had written, asking me to do my old role on "The Clue." I had no idea what was to happen in the old home town.

Beside himself with pride and importance, my father was Mayor Jimmy Walker welcoming Marie of Rumania. No sooner had we reached the house than local TV columnists, alerted by him (possibly threatening to cancel his tire ads), called for interviews.

I had relished the idea of facing my former enemies in broadcasting. But there was no sweetness in revenge. Capitulation was too sudden and too complete. The head time salesman, who'd forbidden his minions to find "Greenbaum's Gallery" an advertiser, took me to lunch, telling me that he'd always said I was years ahead of Buffalo. He had a basement full of films on fly fishing, fifty hours of it, and was ready to do a network fishing show with himself as M.C.

A local sports announcer followed my father and me into a restaurant, looking desperate. "I belong in New York," he blurted. "Do you think Dave Garroway invented looking away from the camera before the red light goes out? Hell no! It was me. Me! Me! Me!"

But truly rewarding was the quiet pride of those who'd had faith in me: Ray Wander, Maurice and Honora Simon, Nora's brother, Paul Zackheim, my brother-in-law Everett, and, down at my father's store, Henry and Lou.

Trouble in Jefferson City

The fondness Jim Fritzell and I had for one another was primarily based on what the combination was able to produce. Away from work, we had little in common. Jim was a man's man, living for sports news, poker games, drinking, smoking, and favorite bars. His talent on a higher level than his taste, he had no interest in theater, science, travel, literature, or music. He watched TV endlessly, preferring quiz shows and old cowboy pictures, even when superior British drama was available. Feeling great kinship with the average American—the hardhat, the serviceman, the minor-league baseball player—he had a finely tuned ear for their dialogue. He put stories together like an honest mason laying rows of bricks. To Jim, our profession was a trade, like plumbing or roofing. When asked what he did, he replied, "Oh, I'm a writer here in town."

The most generous man I've ever known, he was a lending institution which never closed or required repayment from any unemployed actor, writer, or producer *manqué*. Women as sisters and mothers or wives of friends were quite understandable to him, but as objects of desire they became remote, mysterious creatures. One had to use all sorts of subterfuge dealing with them, speaking in a flattering, chiding way, to which they usually replied, "Oh, you!"

In Jim, the talent/neurosis syndrome raged beyond control. With more phobias than a whole passel of nervous Jews, he feared subways, trains, ships, airplanes, crowds, strangers, walking outdoors, and, above all, heights. His phobia-directed behavior was irrational. Often, when it was necessary for us to go half a block from one place to another, we took a cab, digressing two miles because of one-way streets. Once I discovered that even though he took great interest in elections, he never voted, though he pretended he had. "Why not?" I asked.

"Oh, you know why."

"No, I don't."

"Because that's how they get your name for jury duty. And the courts are on the ninth floor."

In our second season, the citizens of Mr. Peepers' fictional town, Jefferson City, were holding a large and loyal audience. Jim had spoken of Micheline, a Swiss girl he'd known in California. A model, Micheline was on her way to New York to try high fashion. Like a tornado, she ripped into his apartment, making it her headquarters. She was young, beautiful in a boyish, bony sort of way, ambitious, acquisitive, and wildly kinetic, moving like lightning every waking moment. Jim was a person of quiet beers and sports pages, completely sedentary, almost Oblomovian. Humor was his forte, a thing which Micheline neither understood nor cared to have explained. And so they were married. Taking a few hours off from the writing mines, we eloped to Elkton, Maryland. My duties were driving and serving as a dazed but dutiful best man.

No sooner had we returned to New York than Jim's modus vivendi changed. They moved from his comfortable midtown second-floor apartment to a high rise near Gracie Square. From franks and beans at Joe's Third Avenue, he began dining nightly at L'Aiglon. The gangling lad, who'd only two years previously lived in a garage in North Hollywood, riding trolley cars, now began paying thousand-dollar lingerie bills from Saks.

Micheline succeeded almost immediately in the world of high fashion. She made new friends, people Jim couldn't stand. He began telling me, through clenched teeth, how happy he was. Three times a week, he took an hour off to visit an analyst. Occasionally he'd return chortling with pleasure. Doc had made a major breakthrough. It was always something like . . .

"I'm full of guilt because I'm taller than my older brother. Hence . . . the acrophobia."

Doc convinced him that all illness was psychosomatic. In one blow, the patient was able to rule out further encounters with two more of his terrors: medical doctors and dentists. He was never to return to these professionals until seventeen years later, when four of his upper teeth fell out and he had a heart attack.

Despite Jim's troubles, his sense of comedy bubbled up often in our daily routine. One of television's young Turks, David Susskind, sparked much of it. Sitting at his desk in the front office of Talent Associates, he decided to install an intercom system.

We stared incredulously at the sound box on our work table. Unless we propped a book against the spring-loaded switch, he could hear us. He may have simply been trying to improve office efficiency, but we had Orwellian *1984* feelings about it.

"How do you like that little squirt?" Jim whispered. He motioned for me to follow him. We went down to the street and took a cab two blocks to a hock shop on Third Avenue, where we bought a four-string banjo and a bass ukulele. Both of us had learned a few chords in high school. The rest of that day, we played and sang "Ain't She Sweet?" into the intercom. The next day it was gone.

Once, as we were struggling against a deadline, our door opened. David's mother was taking her branch of the Hadassah on a tour of Talent Associates. "This is where my son David keeps his writers," she announced.

We stood politely until the tourists had gone. "Come with me," Jim said. We left the office, put on dark suits, and went to a photographer, where we posed thoughtfully perched on high stools—a photographic conceit popular with *Vogue* magazine at the time. When a life-size print was ready, we tacked it to Susskind's wall. It was reported to our satisfaction that he ripped it down in a rage. I wish I had it now.

Jim's best jokes were bastions against despair. Several years later, David Swift became a successful movie director. Married to his second wife, the former Micheline Fritzell, he was directing a remarkable scene involving hundreds of extras, giant rockets, and expensive special effects. Wanting Jim and me to see him in golden glory, he invited us to the set. We arrived to find David high on a camera boom bellowing orders through a bull horn. Below, on their own canvas chairs, were the Swifts' beautiful daughters, a nursemaid, and Micheline. "She'll come crawling back," Jim said.

Halfway through the second season, the "Mr. Peepers" ratings began dropping. But our troubles were comparatively trivial. Senator Joe McCarthy had begun his inquisition. Many actors we knew were blacklisted. Deprived of their livelihood, they dropped in occasionally, asking to watch us work. Work, of course, stopped, but we hadn't the heart to throw them out. Even more politically naive than I, Jim asked, "Did they really plot to overthrow the government?" Eventually, because of his natural sympathy for the underdog, he, too, would support liberal causes.

The second-year rating decline was nipped in the bud. Fred Coe felt that getting Mr. Peepers married to school nurse Nancy Remington would do the trick. The coming event gave us new material for stories . . . rumor stories, engagement stories, stag party and bridal shower stories, finally apartment-hunting stories. The ratings soared. On the Sunday of the actual wedding broadcast, forty million people watched, an amazing figure considering that the coast-to-coast coaxial cable didn't then exist.

Down deep, Jim and I had second thoughts about the marriage. It made the gentle science teacher less of an odd duck. Moving him closer to the mainstream of life reduced opportunities to show him out of his element, a good source of comedy for his character. But the tide had turned. The show was renewed.

Toward the end of the third season, the ratings began to plunge again, this time inexorably. Jim mistakenly felt that he was somehow at fault. Now deeply unhappy, he sometimes failed to show up. On the few occasions when we hadn't been able to bang out a script, it had been written by two of Fred Coe's best "Philco Playhouse" writers, David Shaw and Robert Alan Aurthur.

David Shaw, younger brother of literary figure Irwin, was always calm, supportive, encouraging, and inventive. He worked with me until Jim arrived after a day or two, once asking if David or I knew of a good lawyer. A friend of his wanted a divorce.

Somehow we finished the last show. The series was dropped. Jim left the Gracie Square apartment to Micheline and moved into a one-room midtown hole-in-the-wall. Fred Coe had optioned a novel he wanted to do as a Broadway play. He offered to subsidize us while we wrote it. Jim said we'd seen too much of one another. He wanted to be alone to think things out. Though Jim was probably right, I would have given up ten years of TV success to have a play open in New York.

One day, while looking through *Life* magazine, I read about the Cleveland millionaire, Cyrus Eaton. Once a year, he invited several of the world's most brilliant men to his place in Pugwash, Nova Scotia, and wined and dined them for a week hoping that one of them would come up with an idea to benefit humanity.

In actual practice, the Pugwash Thinkout, as *Life* called it, didn't quite work out as Eaton had hoped. True, Julian Huxley saw a rare sandpiper, but on the whole, the great men devoted their time to eating and playing croquet for a penny a point.

This seemed a good idea for a comedy. I had a title—*The Wabash Thinkaway*—and an opening scene. It is the last day of the Thinkaway. It is raining. The intellectuals are sitting about, guilt-ridden for not having thought of anything.

Famous Meteorologist: "It's much too damp for this time of year."

Famous Biologist (eagerly): "Have you thought of anything?"

Meteorologist: "No, just complaining. My feet hurt."

The Wabash Thinkaway seemed such an obvious winner, I was petrified with the fear that someone else would think of it.

I heard in TV circles that the ear of a famous Broadway producer was always open to a notion for a play. I had seen his name on a hundred playbills . . . Max Gordon.

Max Gordon: What was he like? I had a mental image based on my moviegoing experiences. He looked like Warner Baxter and he was in the company of a slender blonde in a white silk dress which shimmered sweetly over her navel as they sipped champagne.

When I phoned, the real Max invited me to his office. It was small, in an old business building in the theater district. There were posters and playbills all over the walls, but there the magic of the theater ended. Max Gordon was a regular, everyday person. The famous producer could have fit neatly into my father's gin rummy table in Buffalo. But he was friendly. Moreover, he seemed to like my play idea.

"We'll have dinner at my club tonight," he said, to my astonishment.

Things went badly at the Athletic Club dining room that evening. Mr. Gordon's favorite waiter hadn't come in. My host complained about every course. At one point, the chef had to be summoned from the kitchen for a scolding. At the end of the interminable meal, my stomach was an anxious knot. With a courtly gesture, the producer removed a dental plate to delicately rinse it in a glass of water.

"Okay," he said, "the idea has possibilities, but what do I know. Now you see George."

"George?"

"George Kaufman," he said. Kaufman was my idol. Crystal chandeliers sprouted from the ceiling. Champagne began to bubble. He had a telephone brought to the table, Warner Baxter style. Through a glissando of fifty violins, I could hear him making an appointment for me to appear at the Kaufman apartment at two-thirty Monday.

It was then Friday evening. Could I possibly survive the weekend?

After a bad night, I awoke Saturday morning, burned some rye toast, and sat at my desk. I knew my idea was thin. I had to have more. I found a way to work in a romance with the youngest brain, a historian, and the daughter of the millionaire. After that, my mind refused to function. I jumped into my yellow MG and drove out to Teterboro to look at old airplanes.

Sunday morning, I went to my friends the MacDonalds' for breakfast and stayed all day. After we took in a double bill at the Thalia, I returned to my apartment. There was a telegram from Max Gordon.

> "MONDAY MEETING POSTPONED. KAUFMAN HAS A TOOTHACHE. MUST SEE DENTIST."

I wired an answer.

> "SORRY ABOUT MR. KAUFMAN'S TEETH. THANK GOD, MINE ARE PERFECT."

Monday morning, I received a special delivery letter.

> My dear Everett Greenbaum,
> My number is TR 6-1300. Please phone when convenient. Don't be too sure about your teeth.
> [signed] George Kaufman

Deciding to keep that note forever, I nervously picked up the phone and dialed the number. A gentleman with a French accent was expecting my call. He asked me to come Tuesday at two.

Monday evening, I picked at a broiled chicken from Gristede's, wondering how to start a conversation with George Kaufman. I knew better than to try cleverness with him. Suddenly the music on WQXR was interrupted by a newsbreak. The water tank atop an empty theater had suddenly plunged through the roof, destroying the orchestra section.

I was saved! I had an opening gambit. A bit of theatrical news. Drama. Excitement. A touch of danger. No dependency on laughs.

At one-fifteen Tuesday I took my second shower that day. Putting on my wash-and-wear summer suit, I thought I had struck the right note: rumpled but clean. Outside, on East Tenth Street, I jumped into the old MG, listened for a moment to the happy chattering of her electric fuel pump, and headed uptown to 1035 Park Avenue.

When I gave my name to the doorman, he actually let me park near the portico. Then he told me to take the elevator to the penthouse, where I was greeted by the French accent: a middle-aged gentleman's gentleman. He led me into a split-level living room.

There was George Kaufman. The famous face turned toward me. He looked like his pictures: an elegant, bespectacled gray flamingo. Raising a long, jointy finger in greeting, he said, "Good of you to come, Mr. Greenbaum."

I was ready.

"Say, Mr. Kaufman, isn't it a shame about that theater on Forty-third Street?"

"What happened?"

"The water tank crashed down right through the roof. Wrecked the whole orchestra. Disaster."

"What a pity . . ." He let a precisely correct number of milliseconds pass. ". . . that Jed Harris wasn't rehearsing people."

Both of us were surprised at how much I laughed at this. Of course I was nervous, but it *was* funny and neatly delivered. Kaufman, realizing that a perfect listener had arrived, rose to his feet. He was wearing a shirt and bow tie, highly polished street shoes, silk socks with garters, a silk robe, and no trousers.

"This business of writing plays, you know," he said, "becomes more difficult each year. The reason is because audiences aren't willing to sit and listen anymore. They have no patience with exposition. Why, Mr. Greenbaum, there was a time when they would sit still for fifteen minutes while a maid talked on the telephone. But no more."

I had heard that the playwright was taciturn—a man of few words. But that afternoon, speech poured out of him. He talked about his experiences with audiences. How they change. How the audience reflects what is happening in the world. I listened with ears and eyes and open mouth. Finally, after two hours, he turned to me.

"Forgive me for digressing. Now, what is your idea?"

I told him. He began nodding. I didn't know whether this meant "yes, yes, keep going" or that he was falling asleep. I forged ahead. He rewarded me with a smile on the line "No, just complaining. My feet hurt."

"An attractive idea," he said, "a collector of people. Fellow named Koenigberg suggested it, twenty years ago. We never could finish the second act. It's one of those things that runs into a dead end."

Sadly, I accepted his opinion. After all, in these matters, who would disagree with him.

"Feel free to call me again," he said, as Jean, the butler, walked me to the elevator.

It was a clear, cool summer day. The traffic was light, so I drove along the Hudson, which glinted in the late afternoon sun. There was an aircraft carrier in the river. Pretty girls brightened the grimy banks.

Suddenly, I was strangely happy. I had been treated as an equal, almost a fellow artist, by George Kaufman. All at once I was in the middle of a chain-reaction five-car pileup. With my teeth, I bent the steering wheel of the MG to the instrument panel. My front right tooth was broken in half, but my lips were all right because, at the moment of impact, I was smiling.

Hello, Hollywood, Hello

"Mr. Peepers" was finished. Micheline was divorcing Jim, who wanted to sit quietly sorting things out. My romance with a delightful girl named Hooligan Hart was coming to an end. Having been unsuccessful in trying to interest George S. Kaufman in my play, I now faced the future with no job, a wrecked car, and a new front tooth that gleamed splendidly white but was quite numb.

Julian Claman arranged for me to drop by the Sherry Netherland to meet a real Hollywood agent. Beautifully dressed, rugged-looking, with sparkling eyes and ruddy complexion, he could have been a fight manager who'd struck it rich and hired a classy valet.

"Come out west, kid," George Rosenberg said, "we'll have a meeting. The world out there's your oyster."

I went to California.

My first day in Hollywood, I met two girls. One was the Jewish Girl and the other was the Fruit-and-Cream Girl.

I'd checked into the Park Sunset Apartments along the Sunset Strip. The entrance was at street level. The rooms were in tiers which descended over a cliff. At the bottom was a swimming pool, the social center of the establishment.

The great picture studios were still in their glory, although television was growing quickly. Among thinking people, the activities of Senator Joe McCarthy cast pervasive gloom. But none of the clients of the Park Sunset were in the least troubled. Fringe characters dedicated to the scramble, at any price, up the glass mountain of show biz, many were eager to discuss their plans with a stranger.

Andre Boyer, *né* Artie Klein, stretched like a sleepy alligator at poolside. "I'll get me a white Caddy convertible, and a nice white suit and hat and big white Afghan wolfhound. Then every day I'll tool that thing up and down the Strip, up and down. They'll spot me in no time."

Tanya, heavy of breast and lip, declared, "I'll make it, 'cause I got it. If you got it, you make it and I got it."

Dave, the singer, wasn't too optimistic. His car had been repossessed from the Park Sunset parking lot during the night.

"Let that be a lesson to you," Andre Boyer said, "never park where you live."

Within hours, I realized the importance of owning an automobile in Los Angeles. Without one, you were helpless. I'd become bored with walking around the immediate neighborhood. Restless, unsettled, and lonely, I wandered aimlessly through the lobby.

"Easy to see you're new here." The tall redhead was speaking to me, no doubt about it. She was green-eyed, lightly freckled, about twenty-eight.

"How could you tell?"

"Wash-and-wear suit. And you're pale as a ghost. I'll bet you could use some nice fruit and cream?"

"I'm very partial to fruit and cream."

"Come on." She swept away, indicating for me to follow. Her back was as beautiful as her front. She wore shorts the color of old blue jeans. They were frayed at the bottoms, where her splendid legs ran down to trim ankles and the clear plastic heels of her slippers. She led me to her room.

There she opened a small refrigerator, withdrew a container of half-and-half cream and an opened can of sliced peaches. Inviting me to sit at a small table, she served my treat. It was delicious, but I couldn't help wondering what was going to happen next.

"Excuse me just a tiny second." She disappeared into the bathroom. In a moment she reappeared ... completely naked.

"Look! Just look!" she said.

"Oh my!"

"Would you believe I'm twenty-eight?"

"Never. O God. Never. Never."

"And a real redhead. You can tell."

"I see. Oh yes yes." I rose to my feet, ready for some kind of marvelous violence. It's really amazing how quickly the body transforms peaches and cream into adrenaline.

She held out a cautionary hand. "You can't touch me, not ever."

"Why not?"

"Because I'm engaged to a dentist."

After an hour or so I became tolerably inured to her nudity. We chatted. Her name was Paula. She said she loved to read. Before I left, she gave me a copy of *The Prophet* by Kahlil Gibran. "This will change your whole life," she said.

Two copies of this book had already been given to me by girls. I had never been able to make any sense of it. But this was the first *Prophet* I'd ever received from a naked girl . . . a book to be treasured.

Returning to my room, I phoned for a rental car. No one had ever told me Hollywood had mountains. To anyone from Buffalo, mountains are thrilling. I drove up and down the canyons, exploring winding backroads where plucky folk lived in cottages, often perched on the edges of cliffs.

I watched the sun go down through a layer of gray cellophane . . . smog. Hungry, I drove to Fairfax Avenue. At Cantor's restaurant I had cabbage soup and a corned beef sandwich on rye. By the time I climbed back into the car, it was dark.

Having no place to go, I sat watching a plump girl with long dark hair carry boxes from a van into a small shop. Each box seemed to be heavier than the last. She looked up at me.

"Oy," she said, "this is some *schlep*." She was the Jewish girl. I helped her unload the rest of the boxes. The small gift shop belonged to her father. They sold copper ashtrays from Israel as well as oil paintings of Moses and assorted rabbis.

"What would you like to do now?" I said when we had finished the chore.

"I have an appointment," she said. "You can come if you promise not to make fun." She explained that she believed in the occult. She was on her way to a seance. If I gave my word that I would keep an open mind, I could take her. I agreed.

Soon I was driving back into the hills. Down below, the lights of Los Angeles burned yellow through the smog. But the night air was soft, full of the perfume of flowers.

At the end of a cul-de-sac below the huge sign reading "HOLLYWOOD," we came upon an "Arabian Nights" building. A structure of red domes and minarets, built of some material never meant to weather the ages—plaster or possibly *papier-mâché*.

Inside, people sat in a small auditorium. A woman with a fat back was hunched over an upright piano beating out a hymn. There was scattered singing. Elderly ladies wore summer dresses and hats. Many of the men were the mature Hollywood Sports one saw around the Beechwood area: waxed moustaches, dyed hair, black-and-white shoes, holding straw hats in their laps.

The music ended; the fat-back lady stood, welcomed everyone, and then closed her eyes.

"Is there an Aunt Bunny?" she asked.

"Me." A small woman with pink hair raised her hand.

"I hear a little bell. L says she is happy."

"My niece. Louise! She was run over on her tricycle." Louise's aunt was smiling, her eyes filled with tears.

There were several other such communications. I had no idea how well the medium knew these people. For all I knew, the same messages were delivered each week to the same people. But then the piano lady introduced a guest medium from out of town.

"She's very famous," my companion whispered to me.

The celebrity medium was apparently outstanding in

her field. Her messages brought gasps from the audience, sometimes little fits of hysteria. Her fingernails had no polish on them but were buffed with a buffer. She wore rimless eyeglasses. She was, without question, pure Gentile.

But suddenly she began to complain in Yiddish.

"Zedye!" The Jewish girl jumped to her feet. "I'm here, Zedye!"

The message ended.

The girl was shivering. "My grandfather," she said. "He's fed up with the way things are going at the store."

Then the *mavin* medium talked directly to me.

"You have a very old soul, sir. Tremendous effluvium. Many centuries. If you come next week I will have important information for you."

The girl and I went back to Cantor's for chopped liver sandwiches on egg bread. Then there was some nice affection with promises of bigger things to come on future social engagements. We fully intended to return to the seance the next week, but life became too exciting. I never saw her again.

The next morning, I showered wearing my wash-and-wear suit. Then I put it on a hanger. By noon it was ready for my lunch at Romanoff's with George Rosenberg.

My rental Chevrolet was whisked away by a doorman just behind a black Rolls-Royce, ahead of a silver Bentley.

At his regular table, Mr. Rosenberg was as relaxed as I was nervously enthralled. This, after all, was the watering place of America's royalty: movie stars. Mike Romanoff himself was reputed to be a White Russian prince.

Beautiful and famous faces were everywhere. The small balding man at the next table seemed vaguely threatening, somehow familiar.

"Oh, God, it's Humphrey Bogart," I said.

But George Rosenberg saw these people every day. He wanted to hear more about the Fruit-and-Cream Girl, about the Jewish Girl, and especially about how I'd gotten my suit ready for lunch.

A dapper fellow with iron-gray hair, all English tweeds and silk, smoking a cigarette in a long holder, sidled up to the table. I had seen his photograph many times . . . Prince Mike.

"George, dear boy." His Russian accent was charming. "What a pleasure to see you in my establishment. I trust you are being treated with at least common civility."

"Siddown, ya cocksucker," George Rosenberg said. He was one of these people who could blurt out outrageous remarks with great innocence and charm. They seemed pleasantries.

Like all agents, Rosie was permanently attached to the telephone. Whenever I visited his lush Beverly Hills offices, Dorothy Rivers, his proper secretary, led me to the visitor's chair before his desk and put a cup of coffee into my hand.

Rosie would smile a greeting that meant the phone call was not as important as my visit. He'd cover the mouthpiece from time to time to deliver encouraging remarks.

"You're one of the all-time greats."

"You're a hall of famer."

"You're a legend in your own time."

"Getting enough?"

Much of his conversation was intriguing. Like that of diamond traders, the veracity of Hollywood agents is sacred. For all his freedom of vocabulary, George Rosenberg was unable to say one word . . . "liar." "That son of a bitch misrepresents," he would say.

He was imperturbable. Once a client phoned to say that he was canceling lunch in order to dine with a very important star. "Above or below the title?" Rosie asked.

Restaurants provided a perfect background for his eccentricities. He had been entertaining an English playwright whom he wished to represent. But the writer refused to commit himself.

As they stepped outside of Chasen's, a sleek limousine with two uniformed chauffeurs drew up. The doorman leaped to assist a beautiful woman ... Norma Shearer, at that time a great star.

"Rosie, darling," she said. Rosie embraced her, cupping her bottom warmly.

"Keeping the old buttocks firm, baby?" he said.

"I'll sign!" the writer said. "I'll sign."

Once a year, he took me to lunch at Scandia, another place where he had a special table. He thought I should be earning more money.

"I don't want you selling each script separately, Everett," he said. "I want them to be paying you fifteen hundred a week every week."

"I'm sorry, Rosie, I can't get you a deal like that just now," I said. He enjoyed that. After we had finished our meal, we walked toward the exit. He tarried halfway to hug the hostess, an attractive middle-aged woman.

"Be with you in a second, Everett," he called, "soon as I finish squeezing this lady's titties."

George and Aaron Rosenberg grew up in Hollywood, where their father had a small dry-cleaning shop on Santa Monica Boulevard. They made the deliveries on bicycles. One of George's stops was a mansion where a boy his own age waited for the cleaning delivery. For the lad, it meant an hour or so of baseball and laughs with the rough-and-tumble Rosie.

And so, young George Rosenberg, who'd been sent to reform school after pinching the backside of a teacher at Fairfax High, became chums with Bill Hearst, the son of William Randolph Hearst. Astonishing things happened. As a guest at the Hearst castle at San Simeon, young Rosie became acquainted with the great and glamorous of the world.

While the boys were still teen-agers, the publisher decided to round out their education. He sent them on a tour of Europe. The party consisted of young Bill, Rosie, a tutor, and a urologist.

As a young man, Rosie admired the voice and insouciant style of a singer at the Coconut Grove. He began to hang around Bing Crosby. In time, they became close friends and business associates. When he introduced me to Bing, I couldn't help smiling.

"Kid," he said, "shake hands with the Groaner."

George and his wife, Meta, gave a party for Ethel Merman at Romanoff's. There were several hundred guests.

One of the Vanderbilts turned to Meta. "You know, my dear," he said, "everyone in this room thinks Rosie is his best friend."

George Rosenberg was to be my agent until his death many years later, when I passed into the hands of his protégé, Marvin Moss.

Terribly ill with emphysema, Rosie was taken to the Palm Springs home of Buster Collier. The doctors thought the desert air would give him comfort. Wanting to see him, I flew my little Piper Supercub through the choppy winds of the San Georgino Pass.

Rosie welcomed me with the expression which said his day could now begin. Surrounded by tanks and plugged into oxygen tubes, he could hardly speak. He beckoned me closer. Then, his eyes sparkling, he uttered the last words I would ever hear him say.

"Kid," he whispered, "get yourself a lot of strange ass."

Adventures in the Laugh Trade

Rosie asked me what, as a veteran of a hit New York TV series, I might choose to do in California. "Just name it," he said.

"Write movies!"

"Not a chance. Nobody's looking to you for that. What else?"

The big TV show that year was "The George Gobel Show." Gobel had worked years in nightclubs, fairs, and trade shows. He had a baby face, rural flavor, and wonderful timing. Hal Kanter, a successful comedy writer who had also won an Academy Award for serious drama, presented Gobel with sharp, satirical material in a loose, offbeat format . . . something like the staging of Thornton Wilder's *Our Town.*

This soufflé rose like a demented balloon. People everywhere used Gobel catch phrases . . . "You can't hardly get that kind anymore," "I'll be a dirty bird," and so forth.

Hal Kanter had admired the writing on "Mr. Peepers." He wanted to hire me but David P. O'Malley, Gobel's manager, claimed I'd had no experience as a "joke" writer. They gave me a trial period. The first week I contrived some marvelous jokes.

I was hired. The second and third weeks I couldn't think of a thing. But once again, I experienced the excitement of working on a show which was watched eagerly every week by fifty million people. "The George Gobel Show" was big news. Celebrities vied to appear on it . . . James Stewart, Henry Fonda, Jack Benny. Newspaper columnists begged for jokes before they were broadcast.

We were well organized. With the exception of Saturday afternoon dress rehearsals, we worked a forty-hour week. This began Monday mornings, when I joined Howard Leeds, Harry Winkler, Hal Kanter, and a lovely English lady of uncertain years named Muriel Philips at an office in the San Fernando Valley.

Muriel prepared Constant Comment tea for us. She called me "Mr. Greenbaum, dear." Hal, Howard, and Harry were to become life-long friends.

Back at the Park Sunset, life was emotionally unrewarding. No physical relationship had developed with Fruit-and-Cream Paula. Moreover, conversation with the other inhabitants—aside from discussing their "careers"—was limited to astrology. People were always walking around "on the cusp." I was happiest at the office. Colleague relationships seemed closer and warmer than in New York. Possibly this was a hangover from the early days of the picture business when people trekked two weeks by train to take up a new life in a wild frontier. Everyone worried about me. Had I found a decent place to live? Was I eating properly?

On Thanksgiving, the charming Jeff Donnell, who played George's wife on the show, invited me to her home for dinner. John Scott Trotter, the musical conductor, learned that I had no plans for Christmas. Since he was going east for the holiday, he arranged for me to be his guest at the chic Racquet Club in Palm Springs owned by silent-film star Charles Farrell.

For a non-tennis type with no friend within a hundred square miles, Xmas was far from gala. Among the other guests was a rowdy group of middle-aged men and "starlets," seemingly organized by producer Mike Todd. To an outsider, their fun rang with a moronic thud, but the girls were stunning. One sleek, dark-haired enchantress, Nicol Lopez, threw devilish smiles at me.

One evening, in the bar, I shared a small table with several people, Nicol and her escort among them. With brazen naughtiness, she slipped off a shoe and ran her foot up my leg beneath the table. This, with a level provocative gaze, sent my heart leaping in its stirrups.

I found a moment alone with her to ask for a date. "All right," she said, "if you get me a part on TV first." Depressing. Hardly the basis for a rewarding relationship. I decided to forget about her.

One of our first guests on the Gobel show was Ed Wynn. He was then down on his luck. Having grown up in the same Philadelphia tenement as Mamma, he was a great figure of my childhood. As he rehearsed lines, some of which I had written, I could remember sitting on his lap backstage when I'd been taken to Shea's Buffalo theater to see him. I had an idea for a joke.

"Say, Ed, do you have a hat that explodes?"

"Certainly I have a hat that explodes!" (Who hasn't?)

"Good! Do you know who I am, Ed?"

"Certainly, Everett Greenbaum."

"Rose Goldenberg's son."

"Stop the rehearsal! Stop the rehearsal!"

He told how Grandpop had come from Russia as a boy and gone into the candy business. Goldenberg's Peanut Chews, he explained, had been pulling out American fillings for sixty-five years. It was a wonderfully proud moment for me.

One evening, back at the Park Sunset Apartments I was visiting the nude Paula when she seemed more receptive than usual. The specter of her dentist seemed to dim. But the hospitality was not for me.

"You'll have to skedaddle for a while," she said.

"Why?"

"Someone is coming. Someone I'm having an affair with."

Rage! What did this all mean? Was the dental ruling only meant for me? To smooth my feathers, I was permitted to linger until the guest arrived. Jealousy and curiosity joined forces to overwhelm pride. I waited. Eventually, there was a knock on the door. Paula's lover entered.

It was Nicol Lopez. The Park Sunset was bringing me nothing but grief. I rented a small house in the hills and moved.

Jeff Donnell separated from her actor husband, Aldo Ray. One evening I took her to the ballet and dinner at the Captain's Table on La Cienega Boulevard. When I returned to my house, the phone was ringing. Harrison

Carrol, the gossip columnist, reported that I had been "seen" dating the married co-star of the George Gobel show. "Interesting item," he said. "I'll run it tomorrow."

"If you do that, Mr. O'Malley will fire us." I groveled. "He's very religious."

"All right," Carrol snipped. "You owe me a story." These scandalmongers of the West could inspire terror.

Underlying the move from New York to Los Angeles dwells a subconscious feeling that it is only temporary. A twinge is felt at each step in the tearing up of eastern roots: the closing of a Greenwich Village apartment, the transfer of the bank account, the farewell to New York doctor and dentist.

I turned my body over to a doctor on Wilshire Boulevard. After a year on the Gobel show, I felt I needed some care.

A pretty, soft-spoken southern girl in traditional white smock rolled a basal-metabolism testing device into the examining room.

"Why have you brought Basil Rathbone in here?" I asked. Her delighted response to this feeble joke was rewarding.

"What a nice girl!" I said to myself.

Later, my doctor asked me what I thought of his new assistant. I had spent the morning with George Rosenberg, and was still under the influence of his conversational style.

"Tell her I'm going to bite her in the ass," I said.

He did. For the next year I asked her to go out with me in vain.

We'd written a Gobel show in which a scantily clad young woman was to jump out of a cake. As usual I arrived at NBC Saturday afternoon for the dress rehearsal. The cake jumper was spectacular. She was beautiful, graceful, and self-confident. She was Nicol Lopez.

Swinishly, I did nothing to correct her mistaken impression that I had arranged the job. In her dressing room she rewarded me with a long kiss. I asked her out to dinner.

"Lover, I'm real sorry. But I'm just leaving town for a golf tournament. Wanna see a picture of me playing golf?"

I nodded. She dug into a large hatbox, pulling out an eight-by-ten glossy of herself poised to tee off. The course was perfectly landscaped, her golf equipment top quality, and she was nude.

I kissed her again, aware of the depravity of the scene and wishing my class from Bennett High in Buffalo could somehow witness it. Of course they couldn't, but George Gobel did. Finding me with Nicol made him very cranky. I had displeased him once again.

Wally Cox was as different from George Gobel as chalk from cheese. Wally was sensitive, intellectual, an introspective philosopher. George was tougher, a sort of brilliant Rotarian who related to sports, booze, mother-in-law—the keystones of the blue-collar worker.

Wally and I heard the sound of the same drummer. George and I were at two different concerts. Every time I opened my mouth, I antagonized him.

When I told him I was going to Europe for summer vacation, he announced, "I never go where they don't speak English."

After a broadcast, I said the show had been pretty good. He bristled. "Is that all?"

Once, at a rehearsal, in a particularly jovial mood, I handed out the scripts, adding a pleasantry for each person. When I got to George he hissed, "What are you trying to do? Take over?"

A prodigious drinker, George once complained at lunch that he had the world on a string ... successful show, wonderful family ... but he couldn't get the first martini from the table to his mouth without shaking. I picked his drink up and held it to his mouth. His lips compressed, tightly furious. I'd done it again.

George and Mr. O'Malley were very loyal, but only to one another. Hal Kanter, having made Gobel a national figure, asked for a small percentage of the show. He was replaced by a beloved veteran of the comedy world, Al Lewis.

Hal had ruled with a hand of iron. He made all decisions, especially those concerning comic material. Easygoing Al, on the other hand, listened to everyone, including George's in-laws and people from the advertising agency. We had written a sketch in which a grandfather tells a child he keeps his teeth in a glass of water at night.

"Wouldn't it be better for your teeth if you kept them in a glass of milk?" the child replies.

The man from the agency insisted that we change the line to read, "Wouldn't it be better for your teeth if you kept them in a glass of Double Rich Pet Evaporated Milk?" I refused to cooperate. When I reached my house that evening, Rosie was on the phone. I had been fired.

Years later I discovered that Mr. O'Malley had wanted to get rid of me from the very beginning.

"He's wild and unpredictable," he had complained to Hal Kanter.

"I can calm a wild writer down," Hal had said, "but I can't bring a calm writer up."

Hollywood girls seemed to become crazier every day. Once I went into Schwab's Drug Store for a soda. For sixty-odd years Schwab's had been the home away from home for struggling actors unable to afford Joe Allen's, the hangout of the sometimes employed, or the Polo Lounge, for the very successful.

Sitting next to me was a flaxen blonde with delicate ears ... soft curls falling about an exquisite neck. I racked my brain for something to say. She spoke.

"Oh dear." She turned large violet eyes toward me. "Life here is so hard when you don't know how to drive."

"I'll say!"

"Do you drive?"

"Yes."

"Do you have your own automobile?"

"Yes."

"Is it parked anywhere near here?"

"Out back. Right here. Yes."

"Are you busy right now?"

"No, not at all."

"Would you take me for a little ride?"

"Of course. Anywhere at all."

"You're sure it's not too much trouble?"

"Not at all. I should say not!"

"Then, get me to a hospital. I'm hemorrhaging."

Anxiously I drove the poor girl to Cedars of Lebanon Hospital. Before running in, she gave me her phone number, which turned out to be nonexistent.

Quite another story was Miss Ward, the girl in my doctor's office. Her tremendous dark eyes shone with humor, innocence, and goodness. At length, she began accepting my social invitations. Once, on a Sunday drive, I saw the framework of an old biplane rotting in a field. Wanting to inspect it, I climbed through some barbed wire and over a few wrecked cars. As I gazed into the cockpit, I heard someone move behind me. She had followed me to the plane.

Later, back at my house, I fried eggs.

"Don't think I'm trying to criticize," she said softly, "but they're all black."

"That's okay. That's the way they turn out."

"You musn't eat them that way. Oh, those little old burned-up sorry-lookin' eggs." She began to cry. Imagine, a girl crying about my eggs.

I knew it was time to get married.

I had spent most of my Gobel money on a vacation trip to Europe and a sports car. I was unemployed. George Rosenberg arranged for me to write three scripts for a gracious lady, Eve Arden. I earned ten thousand dollars.

I phoned Harrison Carrol at his paper to repay my debt.

"Mr. Carrol, this is Everett Greenbaum."

"Who?"

"Everett Greenbaum. I owe you a story for killing that thing about Jeff Donnell and me."

"Oh yes. What's the story?"

"I'm going to elope with my doctor's assistant, Deane Ward."

"That isn't anything."

We drove to Santa Barbara, where a judge married us in the police station. All around the room were photographs of terrible automobile accidents. Then we went on up to Carmel and San Francisco.

For some reason Harrison Carrol printed the item in his column. And then it got into Ed Sullivan's column in the Buffalo *Evening News*.

In my father's store back east, Henry Hearn, the manager, had settled into the men's room with the *News*.

"Ye Gods," he exclaimed.

"Get A.G.," someone yelled, "Hank's having a heart attack in the toilet."

My father ran to the door.

"Hank, are you all right?"

"Everett's married," came my wedding announcement.

He phoned me the moment the night rates began. "Ev, I don't know what to say. I don't even know this girl."

"You will, Dad, we're coming east." And we did. Knowing that her closest ancestral connections with Jews were Cherokee Indians, my bride took along an industrial-size bottle of tranquilizers. But everyone loved her, and we returned to our little house in the brown hills of Hollywood.

The Years in El Dorado

I began working, without enthusiasm, on a show called "How to Marry a Millionaire." Jim Fritzell moved to California to write a series for Ida Lupino and her husband, Howard Duff. After two years, it was good to see Jim again. He and Deane became great friends.

The rainy season arrived. Rain pummeled the metal awning of our small patio. Jim dropped by. He was having trouble with a scene. Would I discuss it with him? We took a typewriter and a card table out to the patio. In an hour we had finished the entire script. It was truly funny. The old partnership still worked.

We became a California trio: me, my wife, and my collaborator. With the cooperation of the former, a saucy little blond person was born. We called her Billie Amanda.

Jim and I discovered that in Hollywood, one could live nicely by writing every third script of a series, instead of all of them, as we had done in New York. Ownership plus weekly responsibility could have made us millionaires, but we had seen this lead to illness and divorce.

Our needs were modest by community standards. Jim Fritzell's idea of a good time was a sporting event on television. The Greenbaums were happy watching old movies, rummaging through swap meets, and generally mucking about. In time, I was able to own small single-engine airplanes. Skimming above the smog in warm blue skies was the embodiment of all my childhood dreams played out through long Buffalo winters.

The scriptwriter is anonymous. To this day, the tradespersons in my neighborhood think I'm a root-canal man. But inside this pretender to endodontia is a show-business person involved from time to time with outrageous personalities and alarming events.

Some of these are hard to forget.

The first series we worked on was "The Real McCoys," starring Walter Brennan, a magnificent character actor. Even as a young man, he'd played crusty old fellows in movies. But, in his late sixties, as Grampa McCoy, he reached a large and loving public.

To enhance his portrayal, the actor invented an odd limp. Arriving at the studio each morning, he'd remove his false teeth, scrawling pencil marks on the incisors. They became the tobacco-stained, worn choppers of an elderly farmer.

Irving and Norman Pincus had grown up around the

Alvin Theater in New York, owned by family connections. Norman, the elder of the brothers, was the manager. Irving assisted him and later went into television where he developed the prestigious children's show, "Mr. I. Magination." Long admirers of Walter Brennan, the Pincis (as they were called) moved to Hollywood where Irving, following a long struggle with writers, studios, and Brennan himself, brought "The Real McCoys" into the broadcast schedule.

On the screen, Walter was lovable but difficult. In real life, he was difficult. Having lived all of his life in the most democratic of all professions, he was, nonetheless, quite at odds with minorities.

We wrote "The Real McCoys" for over five years. During that time, Walter never really knew who I was. He called me "Phil." From time to time, he confided in me, generously sharing his wisdom and experience.

"You know, Phil," he told me during our first season, "there are only two good Hebes. Irving Pincus and Abe Lastfogel."

One day, deep in thought, he put his arm around my shoulder. "Let me tell you something, Phil," he said. "The reason niggers smell is that they got a poison in their pores. Can't be scrubbed out."

"Here's a riddle, Phil," he once said in amiable humor. "Why won't a cannibal eat an Italian?"

"Why?"

"They're too hard to clean."

Sometimes a plucky member of the company, director Hy Averback or Richard Crenna, who played Luke, told Walter he was a bigot. Our star had a ready answer for this. "Don't mean a thing." He'd leap into a crouch, walking about bowlegged, dragging the back of one hand on the floor. "Look here. Here's an Irish Ape!"

He was not to be deterred. Late one season, Grampa McCoy came toward me, smiling. I knew I was in for some hot inside information.

"Phil, lemme tell you something. I can tell a Hebe from ten feet away. Know how? By the back! The Hebe back don't curve like ours. It goes straight down."

It might seem that I was willing to submit to this forever. But finally my boiling point was reached.

We had written a show in which Grampa McCoy is treated by a Japanese masseuse. I was fearful that he wouldn't work with anyone from another culture. Everyone said my doubts were exaggerated.

Dawdling at the Van Nuys Airport had made me late for several Culver City meetings. Such was the case on the day of the meeting on the "Japanese" script. As they waited for me, Irving Pincus and Jim decided to teach me a lesson.

When I arrived, they were sitting about the office cupping their heads in their hands.

"What'll we do now?" Jim asked.

"It means a whole new script. From page one. You'll have to work over the weekend," the producer said.

"What what?" I said. "What? What? What?"

Irving raised his head. "Walter says he won't permit himself to be photographed with a Jap."

White rage fogged my vision. "I'll kill him," I said. "I'll choke him to death." I ran out the door, heading for the set. They followed me, shouting. "It's a joke! Come back, it's a joke!" One of the brothers caught me. Norman was a very fast Pincus.

Even though I finally understood that the whole thing had been a prank, my anger toward Walter Brennan refused to abate. I couldn't concentrate on the meeting and couldn't eat dinner that night.

The audience watching a successful TV show in one evening is larger than the total audience for the entire run of a motion picture. An actor appearing weekly in a series receives overwhelming fame and adulation. If he appears in a public place, mobbing is possible. New friends come out of the woodwork. Hangers-on tell him that he alone is responsible for the popularity of the show; never mind the writers, the other actors, the director, producer, and film editors.

Now, since he is well known, he gets offers to appear in motion pictures and plays, the things he has always wanted to do. But, instead, he is a prisoner in a dark, drafty TV sound stage for sixty hours a week.

His agent and business managers step in. The actor is unhappy. More money is demanded and granted. The unhappiness persists. New demands! A lush dressing room. More time off. And so forth.

This is the injustice syndrome.

On "The Real McCoys," Kathy Nolan, who played Kate, had it bad. After several years on the show, she refused to renew her contract unless she got even more money, script approval, and the opportunity to direct. Irving Pincus called us in.

"Boys," he said, "at the opening of the next show, Grampa and Luke have just returned from Kate's funeral. Go home and write it as fast as you can."

As we went out the door, he stopped us. "As long as you're at it, let's drop the kids. Little Luke can be away in the Army and Hassie's off to college."

I'll never forget the opening line we wrote for the next script. Grampa McCoy and Luke come in the front door. "I just don't understand it, Grampa," Luke says. "It all happened so fast!"

Our next job was writing "The Andy Griffith Show."

We found perfect harmony with executive producer Sheldon Leonard, producer Aaron Rubin, and Andy. It was the first time we had worked with a star who participated in script meetings. At these, he was not only an asset in the creative process, but his presence made them joyful events. Basically Andy is a small-town southerner, happiest on the marshes with his rifle and hunting dogs. Like my wife, Deane, he brims with that southern rural humor, which in its knowledge of the human condition is very sophisticated.

The morning we met, I'd gotten up early, flown my plane to Riverside for some hardware, installed it in my workshop, and written with Jim. "My Lord, Everett," Andy said, "you are surely an active Jew!"

Jews were something new to him. His reactions to us always tickled me, especially when he married his second wife, Solica Casuto, an actress of Sephardic descent. On his head, a head made for coonskin caps, he wore a yarmulke. On the Johnny Carson TV show, Johnny asked him about his new marriage.

"Ah'll tell you this," Andy said. "One of us is Jewish."

To me he confided, "Ev, ah always wanted to be in a religion where they go to church on Saturday."

He is a large man of large appetites and emotions. Sometimes he laughs so hard he throws himself on the floor. Once, in a domestic disagreement, he hurled a coffee table through a picture window.

In the late sixties, in a little bungalow at Universal Studios, we were writing a movie, *Angel in My Pocket*, for him. I did my Claude Rains impersonation. Andy laughed so hard he punched his fist right through the wall.

As Don Knotts's stature rose on the Griffith show, he and Andy became a sort of comedy team. In all, we would spend ten years working with Andy and Don: first on the series, and later in feature pictures. Andy, Jim, Don, and I delighted in one another. We became close friends.

We had written a show in which a wealthy man, on his way to complete a big business deal, is stranded when his car breaks down. We wanted to contrast the life of this hyped-up executive to that of the sleepy village.

I had recently driven into a gas station with motor trouble. The attendant could think of no cure except to add more gas to the tank. We decided to write such an incompetent into the script. We called him "Gomer" after a writer, Gomer Cool. The last name we took from an actor on the show, Denver Pyle. We had no idea who was going to play the role, but it was necessary to give him a speech pattern. I had always enjoyed the style of character actor Percy Kilbride, and used it as we wrote.

Andy had seen a young singer-comedian at the Horn, a nightclub in Santa Monica. Jim Nabors was happy to get a role on TV.

Gomer Pyle caused a sensation. The character became a regular on the Griffith show. Then Aaron Rubin created "Gomer Pyle, U.S.M.C."

Within a year, Jim Nabors was hobnobbing with movie stars, families of Presidents, and famous athletes. He left all of us behind and, to this day, has never looked back.

As the Bard might have said, "Larry Gelbart is a great doer in our trade." Writer of hit plays and brilliant motion-picture comedies, Larry created a TV version of the motion picture, *M*A*S*H*. He invited us to work on the series.

Another happy, productive five years for Fritzell and Greenbaum ensued. The anchor of the show, Alan

Alda, is a princely, talented man, deeply involved in his family and good causes.

On "M*A*S*H," there were several cases of injustice syndrome, the most severe being McLean Stevenson's. McLean had done well in the part of Colonel Henry Blake, a small-town surgeon coping in the military. But he wanted to be anywhere outside of the "M*A*S*H" set. He wanted to do an act in Las Vegas. He wanted to accept roles in pictures. He wanted to be in a play. Time after time, the script was rewritten so that he could accept some of these offers. But his demands were unceasing. It was mutually agreed that he would leave.

Jim and I wrote his last show. Orders were to arrive, Col. Blake would be given a bang-up party and then ... farewells. In the script meeting with Larry and coproducer Gene Reynolds, the door was locked. The secretary was told "no calls."

Larry took a page of typing paper out of his drawer. "This is the last page," he said. "This one will be kept out of mimeo."

In the scene, the "M*A*S*H" doctors are hard at work operating after the departure of Blake's helicopter. Radar, the little corporal, enters. "There's been an accident," he says. "Colonel Blake's plane went down in the Sea of Japan. No survivors." The doctors and nurses continue operating, tears in evidence above their surgical masks.

Larry directed the episode himself. On Friday, the last page of the circulated script was shot. Everyone was looking forward to refreshments and a small party. It was the last show of the season.

"One moment, please," Larry called. "Now you all know this series is about war. And war is synonymous with death. How often have we really felt that here? I'm going to do something now that'll bring home ... "

The Years in El Dorado 159

"No. No." Gary Burghoff, who played Radar, started to run off. "You're going to show us a dead person. I don't want to see it."

Larry explained what was on the *real* last page. It was shot. In the silence after "Cut!" wild sobbing was heard from McLean's dressing room.

The show created furor. For the first time in TV history, one of the principal characters of a comedy had been killed off. Thousands of letters arrived, half praising and half damning, some addressed to Jim and me. I answered ours, thanking those who had defended the script and explaining to the detractors that "M*A*S*H," although entertainment, was an antiwar show and that the essence of war is the quick and final departure of a loved one. Few of the letter writers, thank God, had experienced such a loss firsthand.

For the last six or seven years, Jim was plagued by heart trouble and alcoholism. But we still managed to meet each day to turn out a few pages. One morning last year, I found him slumped over our work table. He'd had a fatal stroke.

Twenty-seven years ago I was sent into a small office on the East Side of New York City to write comedy with this kind, talented Swedish man. We'd both been listening to Americans all our lives, remembering what was funny or interesting or sad. Our delight in capturing some "good stuff" on paper never diminished. Together, we won many writing awards. More than a partner, he became a necessary relative. Without him, things may be very difficult.

General Frank McCarthy, who produced the pictures *Patton* and *MacArthur*, once hired us to write a twenty-million-dollar production of *Tom Swift and His Wizard Airship*, based on the classic stories of the boy inventor.

He wanted our small-town flair and felt my mechanical aptitudes might come in handy.

Despite the imminent collapse of the big-studio system, preparations for this never-to-be-made picture proceeded full blast. Jim and I finished two drafts of the script. Two Wizard Airships were built by the Boeing Company in Wichita, Kansas.

Gene Kelly was hired as director. In the middle of winter, I was sent to New Jersey to join him. We were to seek out a location where a large set would be built for Tom Swift's dirigible base. We had never met.

Arriving late at night at a hotel in eastern New Jersey, I was directed to Kelly's room. I knocked.

"Come."

I entered. A stout bald man about my height was unpacking. When I saw the scar on his cheek and heard the voice again, I knew it to be "himself." He proved to be a hard worker and genial companion.

The next day, we put on hip boots to hike across a large field. Glacial wind picked up snow, hurling it, bitter cold, in our faces. The snow became deeper. Soon it was up to my chest.

"Gene," I gasped, "the snow is too deep. I've got to stop."

"Gotta keep going, Ev," he said. "That's why we get the big money."